SET FREE!

MOLLY D'ANDREA

DEDICATION

*To the Glory of God who saw
something in me He could develop and use
to help bring hope and healing to others.
Thank You Lord.*

ACKNOWLEDGMENTS

My very special thanks go to the following:

To my husband, Bob, who supports me in the call that God has placed on my life in ministry to those who have walked through sexual addiction and want to be set free.

To my son, Bodie, who has encouraged me to do what the Lord has spoken to my heart.

To my daughter, Yolanda, who knows when to give me a Scripture to encourage me.

To my parents, Fate and Edith, who introduced me to my Savior, the Lord Jesus Christ.

To my sister, Barbara, who is my intercessor.

To Linda, my assistant, who encouraged me to publish this book.

To my pastors, Mike and Gail Thomas, who support me in love and wisdom.

Contents

INTRODUCTION

*E*very day I hear the heart-rending stories of men and women who have been sexually wounded. I often wonder, "How did they survive the scars of their childhood?" Or, "What would my life be like if I had experienced the same trauma?"

Each week on our television program, *SET FREE IF YOU WANT TO BE*, we interview men and women who know first-hand about pornography, rape, incest, sexual molestation and homosexuality. Many of their documented stories are included in this book. You will meet:

- Warren – a preacher's son who developed full blown AIDS.
- Miriam – who became a lesbian after being molested by a family friend at the age of six.
- David – an actor who cruised the streets of Hollywood to find satisfaction.
- Stephen – whose gay lifestyle led to drugs and depression.
- Kim – who was sexually violated by her older brother.
- Dan – how the emotional neglect of childhood led to sexual perversion.

Plus many more.

Like millions, you may have the opinion, "Once gay, always gay." Or, "A person who has been molested as a child can never completely recover."

On these pages you will discover that not only can a person be liberated from the past, they can *stay* free!

You will also learn:

- What God says about generational sin.
- How our actions are transferred into the lives of those we touch.
- What Jesus said regarding same-sex relations.
- How the Lord forgives those who have committed sexual sins.
- Seven steps to *staying* free!

If you are expecting a volume filled with condemnation and judgment, this is not the book for you. Instead, I pray you will feel the love and compassion the Lord has placed in my heart for those who have been sexually wounded.

God, in His infinite wisdom, knows exactly what we need, and *when* we need it. I believe He has placed these words in your hand for a reason.

Will you receive what the Lord has for you?

– Molly D'Andrea

1

"Set Me Free!"

Hawaii is a long way from Largo, Florida, but that's where we decided to go for a few days of rest in November, 1992.

Once morning, while taking a brisk walk on Diamond Head Road, something occurred that I was hardly prepared for. Suddenly, the Lord distinctly spoke to me, asking, "Do you see all these people coming toward you?"

Immediately, I replied, "Yes, Lord!" In reality, there were very few people on the road. What God was showing me was a vision.

He continued, "What kind of people are they?"

Without hesitation, I replied, "They are homosexuals."

"Those are the people I am calling you to minister to," said the voice of the Lord. And He instructed me to write the vision down.

I rushed back to the hotel, found a pen and paper, and began to write: "I am sending you into a ministry to those who want to come out of homosexuality and those who are sexually wounded."

God gave me this Scripture "The law of the Lord is perfect,

converting the soul: the testimony of the Lord is sure, making wise the simple" (Psalms 19:7).

"When is this going to happen?" I wondered. The Lord answered, "Not yet."

A New Challenge

God has unusual ways of getting our attention. He sent two men into our lives who were florists and decorated our home for Christmas. They were extremely outgoing, talented and artistic.

Over time, as the Lord allowed us to become good friends, I wondered, "How can I make a difference in the lives of these people?"

Not long after this time, we were introduced to a young woman who was a lesbian. We began to pray with her and she was gloriously delivered. She enrolled at a Bible college in Oklahoma, and was called by God into the ministry – abandoning her lesbian ways.

We also met Keith, an outstanding young man who had been a drag queen on the streets of Tampa, Florida. He spent years as a male prostitute in the gay lifestyle before giving his life to Christ.

When we learned of the relationship Keith had with his family, our hearts reached out to him. My husband Bob and I felt led to send him to Bible School, which gave him a stronger foundation for his future.

Even before God spoke to me in Hawaii, He was preparing me for the work ahead.

Bob and I promised the Lord we would minister to *all* of His children – regardless of their economic background, racial heritage or sexual orientation.

Like Petrified Wood!

Three months later, in February, 1993, we were invited to attend a meeting in Spring Hill, Florida, being conducted by an evangelist from South Africa, Rodney Howard–Browne. I had never heard of him, yet several pastors shared glowing reports of his meetings.

Bob and I were seated on the platform. My eyes were closed in prayer and I was unaware the guest speaker had entered the church. There was no fanfare or big welcome – all I remember was the awesome presence of the Lord and an atmosphere of peace and worship.

As Rodney began to preach I was seated with my hands clasped together. The reason I remember it so well is because a few minutes later, when I tried to unclasp them, my hands would not budge. They were locked like petrified wood!

> *As the service continued, I felt a fire in my hands, similar to hot oil, and I could not pry my fingers apart.*

Clearly, the Lord began to speak to me. He confirmed, "I have anointed your hands to pray for those in the homosexual lifestyle that they will be set free, if they want to be."

For one hour and forty-five minutes, my hands remained in that position before I could separate them.

"Lord, is it now?" I wanted to know.

He assured me the time was not yet.

Marching Orders

Rodney Howard-Browne traveled to Australia and returned

the next month to a church in Lakeland, Florida. We attended the meetings and the same thing happened – this time in my feet.

During the service the Lord showed me a second vision. There were thousands of men dressed in white shirts with their sleeves rolled up, each one shouting, "I want to be set free! I want to be set free!"

As I moved closer, these men with thin faces would try to raise their hands higher than the person in front of them. Their arms were extended as they tried to reach God. I could not discern what nation they were from; I only heard their earnest cries, "I want to be set free!"

Later that night, after returning home from the meeting, as I was about to fall asleep, God spoke, "It is time. Tell your friends and those in other nations that Jesus loves them. Tell the homosexuals, 'If you want to be set free, you can by the power of God.'"

There could be no hesitation, no delay. God had given me marching orders.

He continued, "I want you to call a meeting for those involved in ministry who are struggling with homosexuality and sexual addictions."

"Yes, Lord. I will do that," was my instant response. My husband and I had a daily television program.

We announced on our telecast that a meeting for people in the ministry who are in the homosexual lifestyle would be held in the chapel of our network. It was designed for those who wanted to be set free. The chapel was packed.

Before the gathering, several asked, "Molly, do you mean this is happening to those behind the pulpit?"

Yes. Any person who misses the mark with God – and that includes minsters – can be overcome by iniquity.

God did a wonderful work that afternoon. It also launched a mighty ministry that has touched the lives of many thousands around the world.

Looking for Answers

Every direction you turn, there are people with needs – whether financial, medical, relational or spiritual. I have needs, and so do you.

Here is what is so sad. Because of what Scripture says about same-sex behavior (Leviticus 18:22), many Christians have withdrawn and avoided these people. Ministers are guilty of lashing out, and even making fun of those who are called "gay." My heart has always been hurt when I hear people emulate them.

When men and women have problems, regardless of what kind, they are looking for answers, not accusations.

My heart grew heavy as God dealt with me to go into this ministry. I began to cry and pray for these precious people – believing that a Merciful Father would transform them if they wanted to be changed.

We don't need condemnation; that's what Satan does. Instead, we need to speak the truth with love.

In a world that is dying for love, where are those with hands to feed and hearts to heal? Why have we criticized so quickly and cast people aside?

"Shame on Us!"

After following God's leading and starting the ministry, I

received a letter from Christa, a girl who had been delivered from years of entrapment in lesbianism.

Immediately, I contacted the pastor of her church to verify her conversion. I learned that Christa had been set free, but had almost no fellowship within the Body of Christ.

Do you wonder why I say, "Church, shame on us!"

More than once I have heard Christians say, "Set free? That sound's good, but I'll just sit back and watch them for a while? They will drift back to their former life. It is something they just can't stay away from."

We need to stop pointing fingers and examine our hearts. It is time to fall on our knees and cry out with compassion – and learn how to effectively minister to these people.

Haven't there been times when you wanted someone to believe with you – to feel what you feel and hurt where you hurt?

Homosexuals, lesbians and the sexually wounded are suffering and the church has discarded them. Even worse, we have little to offer because we have not studied the Word of God and do not know how to reach them. Instead, we mutter, "Poor things!"

What would be your response if a member of your family was attacked by the enemy? For example, what if someone you dearly loved was about to commit suicide?

I hope you would roll up your sleeves and say, "Devil, I have had it with you! I'm not going to let you take the life of my friend."

Would you start a prayer chain, building a protective hedge against the enemy? Would you begin to quote Scripture and plead the blood of Jesus Christ over the situation?

God hears the prayers of His people and can set the captive free!

Join the Battle

Don't sit in your ivory tower of judgment, saying, "God can't use that person because of their past."

While you are accusing, there may be a revival you are missing. Immerse yourself in the Word of God – put on your armor and join the battle (Ephesians 6:14-17). You need:

- Your loins gird about with truth.
- The breastplate of rightcousness.
- Your feet shod with the preparation of the gospel of peace.
- The shield of faith.
- The helmet of salvation.
- The sword of the Spirit.

Now you are ready to walk with the fruit of the Spirit evident in your life: "...love, joy, peace, longsuffering, gentleness, goodness, faith, meekness, temperance" (Galatians 5:22-23).

Jesus says, "Go ye into all the world, and preach the gospel to every creature" (Mark 16:15). We are to "Go out into the highways and hedges, and compel them to come in" (Luke 14:23).

I am convinced that God intends for the last-day revival to be one-on-one.

The Lord uses men and women to teach us, but we can also reach the sexually wounded by personally sharing Jesus Christ.

How will they know us? What is our life saying every day as we live it before the world? Paul declared, "Ye are our epistle written in our hearts, known and read of all men" (2 Corinthians 3:2).

They will know us by our love.

There is only one message. Jesus said, "I am the way, the truth, and the life: no man cometh unto the Father, but by me" (John 14:6). And "If the Son therefore shall make you free, ye shall be free indeed" (John 8:36).

God's Laws

There are millions trapped in sexual addiction, longing for freedom. Even those who have found a church that justifies what they believe have told me, "They preach love, but I have found no lasting peace."

Why is this true? Because when missing the mark with the Almighty causes us to operate outside the laws of God, the satisfaction is likely to be temporary. As Paul the Apostle told the believers at Ephesus, we must, "keep the unity of the Spirit in the bond of peace" (Ephesians 4:3).

Every day I rejoice in the fact that He is enlightening, delivering and setting people free.

In this book you will hear – in their own words – the stories of men and women who have, through God's help, been able to unlock the shackles of their sexual wounds and addictions.

It is my prayer that you will read these pages with an open heart, an open mind, and allow the Lord to guide your steps. Ask for the Holy Spirit's leading – and be aware of the direction He may be nudging you.

2

BREAKING
THE CURSE

A network television program followed the life of an adopted young man who spent years trying to find his real father. Finally, after locating the town and the address of his dad, he was driven to the house.

The cameras were rolling the afternoon his car arrived – at almost the exact same time the father pulled into the driveway.

Nervously, the young man walked up and asked, "Are you Bill Weaver?"

"Yes, I am," answered the man,

"Well, I've been looking for you for years," said the son. "I understand you are my father."

The man's face flashed with anger. He snapped, "Yes, I may be your biological father, but that was it!" He pointed his finger at his son and said, "I have my own life, and I suggest you get on with yours."

The distraught young man turned to his friend and said, "Why am I treated like this? Why does my father hate me?"

He left brokenhearted.

I have prayed with many in that same condition – children cursed and abandoned by their parents.

I am delighted to tell them, "God knows who you are. He called you from your mother's womb and knows your name (Isaiah 49:1). He never creates anything that is unnecessary to Him. The Lord has a design and purpose for your life."

God says, "For I know the plans I have for you...plans to prosper you and not to harm you, plans to give you hope and a future" (Jeremiah 29:11 NIV).

You may have floundered in the homosexual life for years, and wondered, "Could God really love me?" Many say, "Oh, if only my father and I would have spent more time together. If my parents had just been there for me, I would never have been in this condition."

One young man cried, "Molly, I hate this life, but I'm a prisoner and can't get out."

There are many who believe, "Once a homosexual, always a homosexual." Can God forgive, rescue and transform a life?

Many psychiatrists and psychologists believe your feelings and emotions are normal. However, God sees you cleansed and made whole.

The Bible declares, "Know ye not that the unrighteous shall not inherit the kingdom of God? Be not deceived: neither fornicators, nor idolaters, nor adulterers, nor effeminate, nor abusers of themselves with mankind, nor thieves, nor covetous, nor drunkards, nor revilers, nor extortioners, shall inherit the kingdom of God. And such were some of you: but ye are washed, but ye are sanctified, but ye are justified in the name of the Lord Jesus, and by the Spirit of our God" (1 Corinthians 6:9-11).

This is Good News!

Could it Be?

In my search for answers regarding why some people are involved in homosexuality, the Lord directed my attention to the book of Exodus. In chapter 34 these words jumped up from the page: "Yet he does not leave the guilty unpunished; he punishes the children and their children for the sin of the fathers to the third and fourth generation" (Exodus 34:7 NIV).

Could it be? Could homosexuality be the result of the sin of a parent, a grandparent, even a great-grandparent? I began to study the Word on the topic and found that after God told the children of Israel, "You shall have no other gods before me" (Deuteronomy 5:7 NIV), He declared, "...for I, the Lord your God, am a jealous God, punishing the children for the sin of the fathers to the third and fourth generation of those who hate me" (v.9).

I began to think about the hundreds of people who have confided their heart-wrenching stories of molestation by family members – and how it had been a pattern through several generations.

I am not saying this is the *only* reason for homosexuality, but I believe it is an overlooked cause in many cases.

Are you aware of the sins and curses in your family tree? Was there, lying, gambling, alcohol or drugs?

Have the iniquities (sins that are repeated again and again) been passed down to innocent children – including you?

I have heard countless stories of ruined lives because of the sexual sins of parents, aunts, uncles, brothers and sisters. One man wept as he told me, "I didn't go looking for the perversion that came into my life. But it entered and I gave into it."

"No More!"

I learned that my grandfather was an alcoholic and my grandmother was a preacher. My father told me, "When your grandfather gave his heart to Jesus, he took me to the locations on the property where he had hidden his booze. Then we got a shovel, dug a hole, broke the bottles and buried them."

Next, my newly-converted grandfather, stood over the hole and declared:

> *"Devil, I curse you. I send you back to where you came from and I speak blessings upon my children. There will be no more alcohol in this family."*

The curse of liquor was lifted. God says He will show "mercy unto...them that love me and keep my commandments" (Deuteronomy 5:10).

With that as an example, we had a discussion with our parents about the iniquity and transgressions in the history of our family. I am not ashamed to tell you that we called our children together, laid hands on them, cursed those sins and declared spiritual warfare on the enemy.

We did this in order to keep these curses broken from their lives – and so that they would not return to the past.

Stop Blaming Yourself!

When applying for employment, perhaps you have been asked to fill out a form that asks, "Are there any diabetics in your family? Is there any heart trouble in your history? Any high blood pressure? Any cancer?" You may even have been asked, "Is there anyone who has been in prison in your family?"

Why is this information pertinent? They understand that certain weaknesses are passed from generation to generation.

I recall the night a precious young lesbian came to the altar in one of our crusades. When I had a chance to minister and pray with her, she said, "It's no one's fault but mine."

"Was your mother a lesbian?" I inquired.

"No," she answered

"How about your grandmother?"

"No, but I learned that my grandfather was a homosexual," she told me.

"Stop blaming yourself," I said. Then I began explaining to her how the curse could be banished forever.

Reversing the Curse!

Don't think that just because there was sin in your family tree it must remain. No! The Word declares that we can remove the curse.

God says, "For now will I break his yoke from off thee, and will burst thy bonds in sunder" (Nahum 1:13). On the cross, Christ "redeemed us from the curse" (Galatians 3:3).

The Lord can reverse any generational sin that may afflict your life.

How is it possible? Start speaking *blessings*. God says, "And I will bless them that bless thee, and curse him that curseth thee: and in thee shall all families of the earth be blessed" (Genesis 12:3).

If you are ready to be set free, speak to the curse that has been upon you. Say, "Satan, get out of my life! You are not corrupting my bloodline any more. I reverse that curse against me. And now I speak the blessing of the Lord over my life. Jesus wash me in Your Precious Blood and forgive me of all my sin."

Here is what the Bible promises: "That if thou shalt confess with thy mouth the Lord Jesus, and shalt believe in thine heart that God hath raised him from the dead, thou shalt be saved. For with the heart man believeth unto righteousness; and with the mouth confession is made unto salvation. For the scripture saith, Whosoever believeth on him shall not be ashamed" (Romans 10:9-11).

Questions, Questions

Because of our television ministry and crusades, we have received many e-mails, phone calls and letters from people in the U.S. and foreign countries. Their stories touch our hearts and we thank God for the privilege of praying with them. Some simply share problems for which they need a solution. Others have questions such as these:

1. What are the dangers of promiscuity?

Television, newspapers, magazines and billboards constantly warn of the scourge of AIDS, yet I believe there is something just as dangerous affecting the lives of those who are promiscuous and those in the homosexual lifestyle.

> *We need to realize that our actions are transferred into the lives of those we touch.*

For example, a father can come home from work and say, "Don't talk to me. I had a terrible day!"

Immediately, a spirit of discontent enters the household. And if it is repeated day after day that same spirit will begin to operate in you. Eventually, it will *possess* you!

The same principle applies to the homosexual and the active heterosexual. Some promiscuous individuals have hundreds of partners in just a few short years.

2. Are there penalties for refusing to obey God's Word?

Paul explains what happens to those who reject the truth of Scripture. "Therefore God gave them over in the sinful desires of their hearts to sexual impurity for the degrading of their bodies with one another. They exchanged the truth of God for a lie, and worshiped and served created things rather than the Creator – who is forever praised. Amen. Because of this, God gave them over to shameful lusts. Even their women exchanged natural relations for unnatural ones. In the same way the men also abandoned natural relations with women and were inflamed with lust for one another. Men committed indecent acts with other men, and received in themselves the due penalty for their perversion" (Romans 1:24-27 NIV).

There are always consequences for our behavior.

3. What are some of the causes that may lead a person to embrace a homosexual lifestyle?

During the years I have been involved in this ministry, I have heard dozens of reasons why individuals have found themselves in same sex relationships. Here are just a few:

- "I was sexually curious at the time of puberty and innocently began same-sex experimentation."
- "I turned to homosexuality in prison, where a partner of the same sex was available."
- "There was no love or affection shown by my parents. As a teen, I was desperately seeking attention and was exploited by an older person."

"My father had incest with me starting at an early age. In the beginning, he told me this was normal, and I believed him."

- "My friend told me I was just the person he was looking for to spend his whole life with."
- "I went through a traumatic divorce and lost my trust in the opposite sex."
- "I was raped and lost my virginity. It led to my low self-esteem and promiscuity."

4. How do you respond to the person who says, "I can't help myself. You don't understand my urges."

Just because a person has compelling feelings doesn't mean they have to give in to them. Must we condone rapists, murderers and child molesters? Don't they also have urges?

Self restraint is necessary. Paul tells us to "add to your faith...self-control; and to self-control, perseverance; and to perseverance, godliness" (2 Peter 1:5-6).

5. *What did Jesus have to say regarding this issue?*

While Christ did not speak specifically about same-sex relationships, He clearly supported Old Testament law. In the Sermon on the Mount, He said, "Think not that I am come to destroy the law, or the prophets: I am not come to destroy, but to fulfil" (Matthew 5:17). Jesus agreed with what was written in the 18th chapter of Leviticus.

6. *Is homosexuality mentioned as part of the end of the age?*

Paul wrote to Timothy, "This know also, that in the last days perilous times shall come. For men shall be lovers of their own selves, covetous, boasters, proud, blasphemers, disobedient to parents, unthankful, unholy, without natural affection...(2 Timothy 3:3). Do you believe we are living at the end of the age?

7. *What should be the attitude of believers toward those involved in this lifestyle?*

Our view of those who live contrary to Scripture should be like the Father. Because God loves the sinner, He sent His Son to earth. "God commendeth his love toward us, in that, while we were yet sinners, Christ died for us" (Romans 5:8).

Jesus was a friend of sinners (Mark 2:15), and we must be too. He didn't worry about the Pharisees and scribes who murmured, "This man receiveth sinners, and eateth with them" (Luke 15:2).

8. Can God forgive those who have committed sexual sins?

Many say, "How could God forgive me? I have done too much."

Let me assure you that regardless of your actions or how often you have committed the same sin, God hears your prayer of repentance and completely forgives you.

He has fully dealt with all sin through His Son, Jesus Christ. On the cross, He said, "It is finished" ((John 19:30).

God has done His part, and now He offers it to you. "Repent ye therefore, and be converted, that your sins may be blotted out, when the times of refreshing shall come from the presence of the Lord" (Acts 3:19).

The Bible is talking about *you*, when it says, "When you were dead in your sins...God made you alive with Christ. He forgave us all our sins" (Colossians 2:13 NIV)

You can be miraculously forgiven!

9. Is it possible that a homosexual can be set free?

The message of this book is that God can liberate people from sinful practices. Never forget what the Bible promises: "And such were some of you: but ye are washed, but ye are sanctified, but ye are justified in the name of the Lord Jesus, and by the Spirit of our God" (1 Corinthians 6:11). Instead of condemnation, there is hope.

We have friends who have been out of the lifestyle for more than fifteen and twenty years. They are happily married, have beautiful families and are serving the Lord.

I have seen hundreds of individuals permanently transformed by the power of God, leaving their past life behind.

They have been set free!

Starting Over

When someone tells me, "I was born like this," I don't argue whether it is genetics or choice. Rather, I am thrilled to respond, "It doesn't matter. You can be born again!"

That is what Jesus told Nicodemus. He said, "Except a man be born again, he cannot see the kingdom of God" (John 3:3).

"How can a man be born when he is old?" the man wanted to know. "Can he enter the second time into his mother's womb, and be born?" (v.4).

Jesus answered, "Verily, verily, I say unto thee, Except a man be born of water and of the Spirit, he cannot enter into the kingdom of God" (v.5).

The moment you ask Jesus to forgive you and cleanse your heart you are reborn. "Therefore if any man be in Christ, he is a new creature: old things are passed away; behold, all things are become new" (2 Corinthians 5:17).

Let Jesus break the curse!

~

You may ask, "Molly, I understand what the Bible says, but what happens in the real world? Can a person leave the homosexual life and never return? Is it possible to be liberated from a past that includes rape, pornography, molestation, incest, prostitution, orgies and masturbation?

In the following chapters you will read the documented stories of men and women whom I have interviewed on our international television program, "Set Free, If You Want to Be." They are living testaments of God's transforming power.

*Brethren, I count not myself to have apprehended:
but this one thing I do, forgetting those things which are
behind, and reaching forth unto those things which are
before, I press toward the mark for the prize of
the high calling of God in Christ Jesus.
– Philippians 3:13-14*

3

SOMEONE ANSWERED!

*W*arren, the son of a preacher, was raised in a small western prairie town. "Mom taught school and my parents really didn't have much time to spend with me or my brother and sister," he recalls.

Life was simple, yet restricted by the fact that the church was extremely legalistic and Warren was expected to walk the line.

Molly: How did you react to such a rigid upbringing?

Warren: I learned all the tricks of putting on the masks of religion, but it really wasn't in my heart. Like a snake, I would slither around to see how much trouble I could get into without being caught.

Molly: I know you became a homosexual. When did those activities begin?

Warren: I was the kid they called "special," since I was musical, but not athletic. Baseball and football weren't for me. Then, at the age of nine I began fooling around with some neighborhood boys – and the play turned sexual. It became a regular occurrence.

Molly: Were those feelings temporary, or did they persist?

Warren: By the time I was fifteen, I had totally rebelled against my parents, my religious upbringing and life as I knew it. Before long I left home, got a job and moved into my own apartment.

> *About the same time I began smoking, drinking and experimenting with drugs. Even more, I became obsessed with my desire to be with a man.*

I didn't try to analyze what had brought me to this point, or why I had developed such habits and cravings.

Molly: Did you consider moving back home?

Warren: No. I joined the service at seventeen and was determined to find what I was looking for – even if I didn't know what it was! By this time I was sliding down a long path toward destruction.

I was fortunate to receive an honorable discharge from the military, since my superiors were suspicious of my homosexual activities. In the civilian world, however, I soon became an emotional wreck – drinking heavily, smoking pot, snorting coke and dropping acid.

Molly: What about your spiritual feelings at this time?

Warren: During all of these years I was fully aware of my distance from God. I had walked the aisle in my father's church and made a profession of faith at the age of seven. At this point, however, I knew I was not right with the Lord.

Financially, I was secure. I landed an excellent government job, bought a house and settled down with a "friend" who lived with me.

> *On the outside, life appeared good,*
> *yet on the inside I was running*
> *on empty and experienced periods*
> *of great sadness and depression.*

My whole world fell apart when I tested positive for HIV. Soon the alcohol and drugs became more than a crutch, they dominated my life. I lost my job, my house and my motivation for living.

Molly: Did you think about giving up?

Warren: I was convinced that if I really tried to start over, I could make it on my own. And that is what I did. I joined Alcoholics Anonymous, found a new lover, started my own business, bought another home, and for a few years thought everything was all right.

Molly: Was it true? Had your life really changed?

Warren: I took one drink, and it was the beginning of the end. This time I literally lost everything – including my health. Now I had full blown AIDS and found myself on the street, selling drugs for food and living in a shack behind a gay bar. I was barely clinging to life.

> *People shunned me. I was totally abandoned by my family and friends – even my homosexual friends.*

I called a gay church for help and they didn't return the call. Then I phoned a so-called Christian church and they wouldn't even *speak* with me.

Molly: Where did you finally turn for help?

Warren: Four years later I was sleeping in a filthy bed and spending every cent I received from welfare on crack. Don't ask me why, but I began to watch Christian television programs – and even found myself taping some of them.

I thought, "If I'm going to die in this place, I want something positive to watch." I had seen many of my former friends succumb to AIDS and they were an absolute picture of death and hell.

Molly: Tell me about the programs you watched.

Warren: Even while I was doing drugs, I would be sure to tape one particular program, "Set Free If You Want to Be." It talked about hope for homosexuals and expressed how they loved me – a homosexual, with AIDS! Those on the program were not putting me down or preaching hell fire; instead, they cared. Better yet, they told me that no matter what I had done, Jesus still loved me.

I dialed the phone number that appeared on the television screen and was shocked when someone answered. I thought, "I am in Alaska, and they are in Florida. That's four hours difference. It must be three in the morning there!"

As I listened to the friendly voice on the line I knew someone really *did* want to talk with me. And when I heard the words, "Would you like me to pray with you?" I began to cry.

I can't begin to tell you how wonderful it was to really communicate with another person. For the first time I believed that Jesus would love me, too.

Molly: That's not the end of the story, is it?

Warren: No. I came to Florida to meet with you and the people who said they loved me. It was true! You did.

God has restored my health (with medication and two hip replacements) and I am training for the ministry. It is not an easy path, but He made a road where none existed. I have been delivered through the power of Jesus Christ, and He has *kept* me free!

Molly, let me add one more thought. I believe when we see Jesus and lay our crowns at His feet, I might see the sparkle of a little jewel in your crown with my name on it!

Thanks for loving the unlovable – for being like Jesus and reaching out to me.

~

Repent ye therefore, and be converted, that your sins may be blotted out, when the times of refreshing shall come from the presence of the Lord.
– Acts 3:19

4

THE WOMAN INSIDE

At the age of six, Miriam was molested by a family friend – someone she dearly trusted. Almost immediately, she became a tomboy and played the rough and tumble games boys liked. As she tells it, "Unconsciously I was becoming the very person I was molested by – a man."

As she approached her teen years, she wanted to take on a male, macho image, "because I felt that looking like a girl is what got me hurt. What harmed me was the very thing I was trying to impersonate."

Molly: Tell me about your upbringing.

Miriam: Ours was a large family, but one you would not call religious. We only went to church at Easter and on special occasions. In fact, I found church boring.

Because of what happened at the age of six, I harbored deep anger against my mother. I had told her what happened yet nothing was done. Now I understand the anguish and fear she was going through, and that she didn't know how to handle the situation.

My young mind concluded that women were weak and could be easily taken advantage of. That thought germinated into a lifestyle I pursued with the goal of reducing weakness by becoming a symbol of strength – by acting like a man.

Molly: What was the result of your decision?

Miriam: With little guidance or understanding from my family, I struggled with my identity. It led to more than tomboy activities. My life was soon filled with alcohol and unhealthy connections with women.

The path I chose, however, brought great friction between me and my family. In those years there was little tolerance for homosexuality. I know it brought shame to my family and broke my mother's heart.

Molly: What about you? Did you have any remorse?

Miriam: At first I was somewhat ashamed of my lifestyle, but as I became more involved, I grew bolder and bolder. It reached a point where I was no longer embarrassed and just didn't care what other people thought of me.

As a young adult I had a passion for gay rights and pushed the idea on anyone who would listen. For example, I was a sponsor of the Annual Gay Ball in South Florida, and recruited women to compete for the "Number One Gay Couple of the Year." Of course, I wore a man's tuxedo at the event.

Molly: What was happening inside? Was this the life you truly desired?

Miriam: During these years I struggled with emptiness. Something was missing and I couldn't find answers or peace in anything I tried.

> *There was a war going on within me that I didn't know how to fight, so I gave in.*

Many times I cried out, "God, why did you make me this way?" – even though it was *me* who made the choice to become a lesbian as a way to protect myself from physical molestation.

Molly: What led to your spiritual conversion?

Miriam: In 1994, a Christian man was placed in my path who told me about the Love of God. He asked me this question: "If you believe that God loves you so much that He can change you, would you want to be changed?" I said "yes."

He led me in the sinner's prayer and I gave my heart to the Lord. It was the start of my journey to deliverance.

The man offered me a Bible and told me God's Word held the answers to the issues of life.

It was that unconditional love that caused me to look at the Bible with an open mind. Until that time people had judged me and I had lived with rejection.

Molly: Was there an instant change in your life?

Miriam: No. The devil wasn't finished with me yet. He began throwing temptations my direction, and when I saw myself drifting back into my old habits, I began to fight back, praying and asking God to take this demonic spirit away from me. It was a battle.

Many of the things I used to do began to trouble me and I became convicted about them.

Other situations, including the death of a friend, caused me to turn to the Bible for comfort.

Obviously, the Spirit of the Lord was drawing me. Over a period of time many of my desires waned – including my drinking. I began attending church and realized that Satan had wrapped his tentacles around my mind, my will and my emotions. As I submitted myself to the Lord day by day, the devil's grip on me was severed.

Molly: *What let you know the Lord had finally transformed your life?*

Miriam: God allowed something beautiful to take place. One day, for the first time in my life, I saw my womanhood, my femininity. The Bible became like a mirror that allowed me to see myself.

The Lord gave me this Scripture: "And the vessel that he made of clay was marred in the hand of the potter; so he made it again into another vessel, as it seemed good to the potter to make" (Jeremiah 18:4).

I began to recognize the woman in me and made the decision that I would never sleep with another woman.

Molly: *What is your message to those who may have walked your same path and want to change?*

Miriam: I tell people to stop and take a realistic inventory of their life. If a person doesn't know they are in bondage, they don't know what it means to be free. Once they receive God's liberty they will never be the same.

Speaking from personal experience, I can tell you that many homosexuals don't want to live that way. They are looking for someone to take them by the hand and say, "This is what Jesus did for you."

I give them this message of hope: "Christ can change your life."

Molly: *What is the greatest thing you have received from God?*

Miriam: I realized that Satan used my struggle as a weapon to deceive me into taking on the role of a man in a lesbian relationship. The Lord lifted the spirit of shame from me and bestowed a spirit of glory – His glory.

God led me out of the fire. I am no longer looking to the world for love, joy and peace. I have found it in Christ.

He restored me as a woman, a *real* woman – a woman of God.

~

*Therefore if any man be in Christ, he is a
new creature: old things are passed away; behold,
all things are become new.*
– 2 Corinthians 5:17

5

ON THE STREETS
OF HOLLYWOOD

t the age of nine, David hated his life and more than once tried to kill himself. As he told me, "I was one of those 'sensitive' kids and it affected me deeply that my home was a war zone of yelling and fighting. Many nights I'd hide on the floor behind the couch in a room where no one could find me. Or I would spend the day at the movies watching the same film again and again, becoming a part of the lives of the characters – anything to forget the pain of not being loved."

Molly: Was there any particular incident in your childhood that was a negative turning-point?

David: One of the great traumas of my youth was a daily beating by the neighborhood bully. One day I decided to try to make him laugh so that he wouldn't hit me by doing a strip tease. It worked! That was when I discovered that I could get people to like me by taking off my clothes – a lesson that would lead me into prostitution.

Molly: *What was your relationship with your father?*

David: I knew my father only as a fearful disciplinarian. One day, as he was whipping the daylights out of me with his belt, I vowed my hatred for him and declared in my heart that he was not my father.

> *Self-hatred became the natural fruit of that decision, as well as an inability to find my masculine identity.*

By then, masturbation, often before a mirror, had become obsessive. With no one to turn to, I became introspective and an ambivalent narcissist, spewing words of self-hatred into the mirror every day after school.

Molly: *How did you relate to women?*

David: From my earliest years, a lady in our family environment, who looked like Marilyn Monroe, would incessantly tease me about girls. I grew up with a deep internal fear that a mature woman would humiliate me.

Over many years, my parents were not happy with one another and I became my mother's emotional surrogate. For example, I was the only one of four boys who was allowed to travel with her on a train trip to Florida. Though the relationship was never overtly sexual, a deep river of confused sexuality ran through those moments of closeness with her.

Because of my fear of mature women, I chose to see

them as sexless "Snow White" figures.

When I became sexually active in my late teens, it was far less stressful to spend time with males. Besides, most of the ones who came after me were older men who didn't expect commitment or reciprocation on my part. Deep inside I was still looking for "Father Knows Best," and when older men gave me the time and attention that I craved, the results were almost inevitable.

Molly: Did you have any spiritual experiences as a young person?

David: I did have one moment of knowing the presence of Jesus during my formative years. A woman in our church was singing "O Holy Night," one Christmas and the presence of the Lord filled the sanctuary. That hour seemed exquisitely beautiful, yet I had no relationship with the Lord that allowed me to carry it forward. Except for that moment, I grew up hating God. My father, being a minister, cast an unholy image of God the Father for me, and I hated them both.

Molly: I know that you eventually moved to Hollywood. What led to that decision?

David: When the opportunity presented itself to indulge in pornography, I was more than happy. Yet as I looked at the pictures, I would say to myself, "I can never attract a girl like that, I don't have a body like that. I'll never be able to do the things those people are doing." And so it was that even heterosexual pornography sent me deeper into homosexual confusion.

By my late teen years, I was catapulting headlong toward the gates of Hell – never expecting to live to see my 21st birthday. I became extreme and reckless with everything I did, indulging in a drug habit that would have killed most people. At some unconscious level, I had concluded that I was too far gone to ever be rescued, so I set out to re-live Errol Flynn's life, as chronicled in his book, *My Wicked, Wicked Ways*. Deciding to let fate take me where it might, I moved to Hollywood.

Molly: *How were you received in the movie capitol ?*

David: To everyone's amazement, within a very short time I was landing roles in movies. My internal cauldron of fury and anger gave me an ability to communicate deep emotion on the screen. Before long I was represented by two of the best agents in town, appeared in a slew of national commercials and had two starring movie roles under my belt. My new-found friends were telling me, "You're going to be the next James Dean." Yeah, right!

Molly: *Where did the acting career lead?*

David: What no one knew was that I was leading a double life. By day I was what the teen magazines called "a rising star," vying for leading roles with the young actors of the day. At night, however, I was "Steve" – a hustler on the streets of Hollywood, hitchhiking my way up and down Sunset and Santa Monica boulevards, subconsciously trying to destroy the success that I was having because I did not feel I deserved it.

Some nights I would weep as I stood on the curb waiting for someone to pick me up, wanting to just be normal. Often I would get into cars knowing my life might be in jeopardy – and hoping they would just get it over with quickly. Looking back, I believe the God I lived to hate was giving me the chance to exist for another day.

Molly: How was your life finally turned around?

David: This went on for about seven years before God made His move. I'd been following a guru for about a year, when the Lord compelled me to visit Israel. It was there, in the Garden of Gethsemane, He spoke and said He loved me so much that He died on the Cross for me.

> *Yes, me – the one who hated God,*
> *the drug addict, the homosexual,*
> *the prostitute – He loved me.*

At that moment I realized what the bottom line of life really was; it was loving God with all our heart, soul, mind and strength because He first loved us. He proved it on the Cross two thousand years ago. Everything else suddenly became meaningless.

Molly: How did your decision to follow Christ change your homosexual desires and activities?

David: It has been over twenty years since my conversion. God has been faithful to continue His unfailing love and commitment toward this sinner. He has won my heart by love and He has won my obedience by grace.

He has fathered me and drawn out the latent heterosexuality that has always been there. He has removed my fear of women and given me a healthy view of both sexes. The Lord has also shown me how to put to death the idolatry that lies deep within my heart and which was the fuel for my life of sin.

Molly: *What happened to the relationship with your father?*

David: I thank God that He enabled me to forgive my father, with whom I had a marvelous reconciliation two years before his death. The Lord has shown me how to bury the old remnant rebel, how to hate my past wicked ways, and how to love holiness and righteousness.

The Lord has given me the intimacy, love, and peace my heart always longed for. He will do the same for anyone who calls upon Him.

~

For sin shall not have dominion over you:
for ye are not under the law, but under grace.
– Romans 6:14

6

A CRY FOR HELP!

Stephen was attracted to men from the age of seven. "I didn't know about sex," he says, "but I found myself eyeing men on television, especially when they had their shirts off or were wearing tight trousers."

By the age of thirteen, he had his first homosexual experience with a willing older man. Explains Stephen, "I was naive, but with time I grew more experienced and enjoyed looking for men to have sex with at every available moment."

Molly: Did your schoolmates know you were a homosexual?

Stephen: At junior and senior high school I was ridiculed on a daily basis for being different. I was laughed at, spit upon, tripped in the hallways and even beat up. Sometimes even the teachers took part in laughing at me.

Molly: What was it like around your home?

Stephen: At home, my mother, sensing a difference in me, started mentally and emotionally abusing me. After a day of jeering at school, I came home to the rejection of my own mother – whom I looked to for the love and support I so desperately needed.

Molly: *What effect did this have on you?*

Stephen: After several years of constant abuse, I developed a severe inferiority complex. I would stay to myself and avoid making eye contract with anyone; not wanting to see them laugh at me, or hear them use the word "faggot."

Drugs and alcohol became my method of escape and I began "acting up" in the classroom. It led to a daily appearance in the principal's office. When I turned seventeen, the principal informed me, "You have the option of quitting school, even without your parent's written consent." Obviously, he wanted me gone!

That was the path I chose – and it was a disastrous mistake. When I came home that day, my mother angrily asked, "What are you doing home from school so early?"

I told her I had quit school for good, and she bellowed at me in no uncertain terms, informing me that I was not going to "sit on my ass in the house." She demanded that I immediately get a job so I could start paying room and board.

In retrospect, I believe if I had been encouraged to stay in school and been shown even a little love and understanding, I may have avoided the tragedy that was ahead.

Today, I take full responsibility for my own actions, but at the age of seventeen I did not have the maturity that was needed to make such important choices.

Molly: *Where did this decision lead you?*

Stephen: The next thirty years of my life was not a pretty picture. I began hanging with the wrong crowd: stealing, cursing, doing drugs, drinking uncontrollably and picking up men by the dozens. Unfortunately all of these activities could not fill the aching in my heart.

Endowed with self-hatred, low self-esteem and a feeling of worthlessness, I embarked on a journey of LSD trips which left me half-crazed and depressed. I soon began to shoot heroin and anything else I could get my hands on to help ease the pain and paranoia that was ruining my life.

At the same time I was in an out of many homosexual relationships, none of which lasted very long.

Being gay, I was hated wherever I went, even by complete strangers, who looked upon me as if I was the scum of the earth. I felt totally hopeless, even attempting suicide. It was a cry for help, but no one came to my rescue.

Molly: What about your parents. Did you turn to them for help?

Stephen: My mother had been successful in turning my father and brother against me, so it was years between visits with my family – and when I did return I was treated with hostility and contempt. This only contributed to my self-hatred.

There were times when I had no other choice but to move back with my parents. It was a terrible situation since my mother would heap abuse on me. On one occasion I was badly beaten by a group of men, and on arriving home bandaged and bruised, she shouted, "Those men should have killed you!" During the Vietnam war she told me she hoped I would be drafted into the service and be killed! Often she said, "I wish you had never been born." My distant father looked on disinterested in my plight.

Molly: Did you ever try to change?

Stephen: The years dragged on with no end in sight. Then one night, after being stopped for drunk driving, the officer pulled me out of the car and I began to cry. The policeman said, "Sir, I think you might have a problem with alcohol, but if you promise me you will get help, I won't write this citation." He called my father to pick me up.

At four o'clock that same morning, I told my mother, "I want you to take me to a mental hospital. I need help!"

"Who is going to pay for it?" was her first response. I explained that I had taken out an insurance policy that would cover it. So off I went to a mental facility in our home state of Pennsylvania.

Three days later, after seeing other people shuffling aimlessly down hallways, not knowing why they were there, I checked myself out. It scared the heck out of me! On returning home I realized I needed to separate myself from my abusive mother if I was ever going to get well.

In 1986 I moved to Florida with a new-found lover to begin what I thought was going to be a fresh start. As soon as we settled in Tampa, I descended into a maze of drugs, alcohol and sex. My partner would ignore me for days after a binge, but he did not hate me more than I hated myself.

Molly: What finally turned your life around?

Stephen: In November, 1995, afer many years of this destructive behavior, I came home after a night of debauchery and, unable to sleep, turned on the television.

Surfing the channels, I came upon an angel, named Molly, hosting a television ministry by the name of "Set Free, If You Want to Be!" Yes, it was you.

Curiously drawn to the name of the program, I watched and was mesmerized by what I saw. I had never heard the words "hope" and "homosexual" used in the same sentence. Then I listened as you told me, "Christ can and *will* set you free from the bondage of homosexuality"

I had always been told by the gay community that we were born that way. Could I really unload this miserable homosexual life?" I had always assumed God hated me because of what I was and did. Now, with compassion in your voice, you were explaining to me that Christ loved me so much He died on the Cross for my sins."

Molly: *What was your response?*

Stephen: For the first time I understood that homosexuality was a sin, not a way of life. That made sense.

After the program all listeners were invited to call in to talk to a prayer partner. I dashed to the phone. Could this be true? Could I, a horrible sinner, be set free from this destruction and avoid Hell – to be cleansed with Jesus' blood and be redeemed? A voice deep inside me shouted, "No you can't be saved. You are too far gone for anyone to save the likes of you!"

I nervously dialed the number, hoping that I was not too late to talk to someone or that this was not a dream. I talked with Ken, a phone counselor, who prayed the prayer of salvation with me.

Molly: What were the next steps on your journey?

Stephen: That was the beginning of a marvelous transformation. No, it didn't happen instantaneously. Day after day I prayed and read God's Word as I turned my life and will completely over to Him.

Scripture told me that if I had enough faith I could move mountains. So I prayed endlessly, "God remove homosexuality from my life." Gradually I lost my sexual addiction to men and He removed the sin completely. I also prayed to be set free from drugs and alcohol and soon the desire for those things also vanished.

In 1999, after seeking out several churches, I finally found a church that accepted me. I joined and was baptized. Daily, I thank God that Jesus has removed my sin and filled me with His wonderful grace and love.

I didn't change myself. Jesus changed me!

～

Our soul is escaped as a bird out of the snare of the fowlers: the snare is broken, and we are escaped. Our help is in the name of the Lord, who made heaven and earth.
– Psalms 124:7-8

7

"Let Me Live!"

To say that Pat had a traumatic childhood is an understatement. She was raped by her father at the age of twelve – while her mother was in the hospital having another child.

"I began living in foster homes when I was fifteen," recalls Pat, "moving from one house to another. The only person who showed me love was my aunt, Dot, and she died when I was twelve."

Molly: What do you remember from your childhood years?

Pat: My brother and I were constantly told how stupid and dumb we were. I believed it when I was berated, "You'll never amount to anything." So I set out to show everyone how bad I really was and tried to act as though I didn't care. But I did. Inside I was a confused, hurting child.

In one foster home I would take their family pictures to my room and play with them – pretending I belonged. After repeating this activity several times they sent me to another home. There, I began collecting photos of movie stars, storing them in different boxes. In my make-believe world, these celebrities became my family. It was years before I burned the collection, knowing this dream would never come true.

Molly: *Did you ever return to your parents?*

Pat: No. At seventeen I left foster care and was on my own. I had a chip on my shoulder no one could knock off.

When I tried to visit my parents, my mother didn't want me around, thinking my dad would commit the same despicable act. Instead, I turned to the only people who would take me in – prostitutes, junkies and homosexuals. I felt especially accepted in the gay community because we had something in common – we had all been rejected.

I saw and indulged in every perverted and twisted thing imaginable. The drugs, alcohol and sex were used in an attempt to mask the rejection of my childhood. Later, after my dad divorced my mother, I tried to return home. My mother was an alcoholic and I thought, "If I mimicked her behavior, she would also love me." Drinking, however, did not bring us together.

Molly: *When did your same-sex activities begin?*

Pat: I heavily immersed myself into a lesbian lifestyle when I was about twenty. And that is how I lived for nearly thirty years!

Several times I tried suicide, even shooting myself at the age of twenty-one. As I lay dying, I looked up to heaven and said, "God, if you will let me live, I will give you my life." He did, but I didn't.

Instead, I returned to my lesbian ways. After my father's actions, I was afraid of men, so I became the aggressive partner, not really wanting to be touched. It reached the stage where I seriously considered having a sex change operation, even counseling with a psychiatrist on the topic.

Molly: Describe your personality during this time.

Pat: I was filled with anger, bitterness and hate – to the point that I was jailed for trying to choke a woman. And once I put a gun in the face of my landlord.

> *On more than one occasion I found myself beating the woman I was with – that's what my dad did!*

Anger and drinking made me crazy, out of control. My temper was so fierce that I would actually black out. On one occasion, my friends told me, I threw a kitten against the wall and killed it! I don't even remember the incident.

Molly: Did you ever attempt to leave the lifestyle?

Pat: Several times, I tried to stop drinking and come out of the lesbian lifestyle, but never successfully. I drifted from place to place, state to sate, yet nothing changed but my address.

At one time I tried prostitution, yet I hated men so deeply I could not continue. Gay men were another subject. I felt safe around them because they acted like women.

I've rolled men for money, eaten spoiled food that was

thrown away, stolen vegetables from gardens and slept on the streets.

Once, in a moment of despair, I met a man in a bar and decided, "I'm tired of the gay life. Let's get married." We were both alcoholics. A week an a half later (after spending a night in jail for fighting) I left, never seeing him again.

Molly: *Did you ever try to reach out to God?*

Pat: I made several attempts to read the Bible, and even tried to convince myself I was born again. It was like a vaccination that didn't take.

Once I pointed my finger toward heaven and said, "If You made man in Your image, you must have been queer, too." Then I tore the Bible apart and threw it in a swimming pool.

I even took communion in a gay church, trying to rationalize it was okay to be both a lesbian and a Christian, but I couldn't make it work. Deep down I knew there was something terribly wrong with being in bed with a woman, and later being on my knees before the Lord.

Molly: *What brought you to a true spiritual experience with Christ?*

Pat: In 1991, in the operating room of a hospital, waiting for a surgeon to perform a hysterectomy, I had reached the end of the line. I looked up to God and said, "Lord, if I cannot get right with you – if I can't stop drinking and being a lesbian – let me die!"

At that moment I asked Him to come into my heart and

to forgive every sin I had ever committed. I meant it from the depths of my soul.

Molly: *How did you know that you were a new person in Christ?*

Pat: All of my life I've known loneliness, and wondered if I would ever get used to it. Well, Jesus has taken it away. He filled me with joy. He also removed my anger and my desire for alcohol.

> *Perhaps the greatest moment after my salvation was when I was able to forgive my parents for everything that had taken place so many years ago.*

All of those events are now buried in God's sea of forgetfulness. The Lord has led me to a wonderful church and has surrounded me with people who live by God's principles. I will never go back to the old life. It holds absolutely no attraction for me.

Finally, I feel like a woman.

Molly: *What advice do you have for those wanting to come out of the gay life?*

Pat: Once, I heard a homosexual say, "I prayed for God to change me. He didn't, so it must be okay."

No, it isn't! God's Word makes that clear. It is an abomination in His sight.

Satan has a counterfeit for everything the Almighty created. Homosexuals are Satan's imitation for what God intended between men and women.

We can never be successfully delivered out of anything that has a hold on us, until we *want* to. When we earnestly desire change, God will help us. Remember, since He gave you a free will, He will never force you. The decision is yours.

~

Let not sin therefore reign in your mortal body,
that ye should obey it in the lusts thereof. Neither yield
ye your members as instruments of unrighteousness
unto sin: but yield yourselves unto God, as those that
are alive from the dead, and your members as
instruments of righteousness unto God.
– Romans 6:12,13

8

LIFESTYLE, OR "DEATHSTYLE"?

John and his male companion decided to purchase a home together and applied for life insurance to cover the mortgage. A few weeks later they received the policies back in the mail explaining they were not insurable with the company.

"That was the scariest day of my life," says John. It could only mean one thing. I must have AIDS. We went to the doctor and it was confirmed; we had both tested HIV positive."

Molly: Take me back to the beginning. What brought you to this point?

John: My father was in the military and was also a commercial fisherman. I remember him coming home every day around 4:00 P.M., changing clothes, then rushing out of the house to do his fishing.

I often retreated to my room, crying because I longed for his attention. "Why won't he spend time with me," I wondered.

59

When I looked out the window and watched the man next door playing with his son, I felt alone and unwanted.

I thought, "What's wrong with me?" What have I done to cause my father to dislike me?" Those questions haunted me throughout my childhood.

I can't even remember my father telling me that he loved me until I was an adult. By that time the damage had already been done.

Molly: How did you relate to your schoolmates?

John: In the fifth grade I began to feel rejected by boys of my own age, because I had practically no skills in sports. When teams were picked, I was always the last one chosen – someone would get stuck with me!

There were no male role models in my life to teach me the things boys should know.

To and from school I always took my time to get to the bus stop. I wanted to be the last one on board and sit in the front – so kids in the back would not make fun of me. My peers began calling me names, like "sissy" and "queer."

I began thinking, "maybe they are right," because I was beginning to fantasize about men.

Molly: When did you have your first gay encounter?

John: I struggled with these feelings all through school. I began to wonder, "How can I make men like me? What do

I need to do to get their acceptance?"

At seventeen, spending a day at Disney World, I met a gay man who introduced me to the homosexual lifestyle.

The first time I went to a gay bar I was immediately accepted and felt a sense of comradery.

> *I was excited to be with people*
> *who actually wanted me around.*
> *For the first time in my life I found*
> *a place where I "fit in."*

I dropped out of school and became lost in a life of homosexuality. It wasn't long until promiscuity began to take its toll. I had several venereal diseases, yet continued to be sexually active.

After a year immersed in this atmosphere, plus the drugs and constant drinking, I felt uncomfortable and abnormal in the larger society.

Molly: Did you accept your new life, or did you try to change?

John: I remember asking the Lord, "Why do I have to be so different? I don't want to live this way." At times I asked God to take my life, and even contemplated suicide.

In an attempt to change my destructive ways, I moved to Maine and continued my education, However, it was not long until I was entrapped in the gay life again – looking for love and happiness in all the wrong places.

I began thinking, "If this is all life has for me, I may as

well make the best of it." So I became involved in a long term relationship and moved back to Florida.

My partner and I purchased a home and applied for life insurance to cover the mortgage. That's when I first learned we had both tested positive for the HIV virus. And for the next several years, I thought about death – how and when it would come.

Molly: What about your spiritual life?

John: Although I knew about the Lord, and made a profession of faith at the age of thirteen, I had no relationship with Him. Often I prayed that the Lord would transform me and allow me to live a heterosexual, productive life. However, I began believing this was a prayer that would never come true because of the lie I had been told for many years: *once gay, always gay!*

> *Finally, I decided that since we both were going to die, I would stay with my partner, At least I would not have to exit this world alone.*

Molly: At that point did you consider totally giving up?

John: No. Although I could not explain it, my desire to pray became stronger. I continually asked the Lord to change me, because I knew deep inside I was living contrary to God's will. As I prayed, the Lord showed me several things:

- That I would leave the gay life.
- That I would help others to exit the lifestyle.
- That God would bring me a wife and a family.
- That the Lord would heal me and I would share His goodness with many people.

At the time, those things seemed an utter impossibility.

Molly: When did the Lord finally come into the picture?

John: In June, 1990, a friend asked me to hear a guest speaker at her church. I accepted the invitation and listened to the story of a man who had been involved in the homosexual lifestyle – or "deathstyle" – for fifteen years. He declared "through the love, forgiveness and strength of the Lord, I was able to overcome my sexual brokenness." He was now married with a ten year old daughter. He also made it clear that homosexuality is a learned behavior, not a defect in our genes.

Molly: What was your response?

John: The message changed my life. I told a friend, "I've made my decision. I am going to leave my partner and trust God for my future."

Committing my life totally to the Lord, by faith I moved out of the house. God began to do everything He had shown me. I was given a second chance at life and immediately began to help others break free from their sexual addictions.

Next, the Lord blessed me with a beautiful wife – a gift beyond anything I deserved. And we have a wonderful son.

The Lord also began the work of restoring my body. Thank God for miracles!

~

That if thou shalt confess with thy mouth the Lord Jesus and shalt believe in thine heart that God hath raised him from the dead, thou shalt be saved.
— Romans 10:9

9

BEYOND INCEST

*A*s a young girl, Kim was sexually violated by her older brother. "Although we were brought up in a Christian home, neither of us were ever taught anything about sex," she told me. It led to incest.

"At the time I thought this is how brothers and sisters acted with one another," says Kim. "I had no real friends to tell me otherwise."

Molly: *What was your response to his aggression?*

Kim: Even though I was totally ignorant about sex, I lived in fear of my brother's attacks. I felt hurt and angry after each episode. At night I would bury my head in my pillow and wonder how I was going to survive the next day.

My brother told me how much he hated me – and how he wished I'd never been born. He often threatened to kill me.

During those years I took several showers a day trying to wash away how dirty I felt. Day after day I felt awful about myself, without really knowing why. And that made it worse.

65

My brother's hate spilled over on me, filling me with fear and anger. I felt too ashamed to relate to others, again leaving me with no friends.

Molly: *How long did the abuse continue?*

Kim: I was twelve years old when my parents took me to a non-denominational meeting held in a local school auditorium. I don't remember the speaker's name, but I will never forget what he said. He spent several minutes talking about sexual abuse, and how the Lord can heal us from it.

I accepted Christ as my Savior. Although I had known *about* God, and had felt His comforting presence when I needed it most, I didn't really *know* Him.

That same night, when we returned home, my brother tried to rape me again. With boldness, I told him, "No!"

I was amazed that he listened to me and stopped. He never again touched me sexually after that.

His contempt and hate, however, continued. He constantly ridiculed my faith in God and he refused to go to church – trying to blame me for his actions.

Molly: *Did your mom and dad know what had been taking place?*

Kim: I was sixteen years old when my parents were finally told by a friend about the incestuous abuse. In complete terror of the retribution that would surely come from my brother, I ran away from home. I spent the next two weeks with my boyfriend at his uncle's farm. My boyfriend (who is now my husband) listened as I prayed in anguish, too afraid for my life to go home.

When I finally summoned the courage to return to my family, my worst fears were realized.

> *My parents placed the blame for the abuse on <u>me</u>! And my brother was livid that my mom and dad had finally learned the truth.*

I was devastated. The pain and torment I had known in previous years began to resurface and drowned the voice of God who had been directing my life. It scared me. I thought, "I'm not even good enough for God to love."

Molly: Did you remain with your family?

Kim: In August, 1990, I married my boyfriend and we began our life together, yet the emotional roller-coaster continued.

Six years and two children later, my husband and I moved to Florida. The fury within me, however, still raged, and we fought constantly.

Many times I prayed, "Lord, deliver me from this anger," yet it persisted. I loved my husband and children with all of my heart and knew they didn't deserve to be subjected to my temper.

Molly: Where did you turn for assistance?

Kim: At a time when my son became sick, I decided to call a local agency for help. In reality, I just needed someone to talk with. The organization I dialed dealt with the prevention of child abuse and they sent a volunteer to visit – to help me find the right resources.

As I got to know the women in the organization, I found a friend I now call "Mom." She realized that it was not my son, but *me*, who needed help.

Molly: What was the result of this encounter?

Kim: Mom brought me through the storm of my anger. She too had been abused and understood my feelings. She was there whenever I needed her, even if it was three o'clock in the morning.

She told me, "God loves you no matter what has happened."

She became a mother in the truest sense of the word – teaching me how to be a good parent to my own children and a wife to my husband. For example, I had never been taught how to cook, clean or do anything a housewife needed to do. My husband did all the work.

With Mom's help, all that changed. She was also my spiritual mentor, teaching me how to serve the Lord and how to listen when He speaks.

God answered my prayers and the gloomy clouds of my

past dissipated.

Molly: What about the relationship with your brother and your parents?

Kim: I vividly recall the day I phoned my brother and told him what had been taking place in my life. It was at a moment when he would listen – he had recently almost died from high blood pressure.

> *For the first time, my brother asked me to forgive him, and I did. It was a marvelous breakthrough.*

My parents also asked for my forgiveness. They came to realize that I did not encourage, nor did I deserve, what happened in my childhood. All of those issues are now behind us.

What a difference the Lord makes. Instead of arguing, my husband and I spend our lives pouring love into our children, building in them a strong belief in God.

Molly: What can you tell people who may be going through a similar experience?

Kim: It is faith that gets me through the darkest days – and Mom and I remain the best of friends. Together we are helping people through the horrors of incest.

My husband and I open our home to kids who are going through tough times – even if it is just for the night. I understand their plight.

What do I tell them? "Don't worry. No matter what happens, God loves you. He will take away the hurt and make things new."

~

Because thy lovingkindness is better
than life, my lips shall praise thee.
— Psalm 63:3

10

"THE SMILING BANDIT"

*A*lan grew up in a home which was torn apart because of alcohol and drugs. "My parents divorced when I was young and I was raised by my mom," he recalls. "She worked hard to make sure that we had material things, but there was little outward display of love."

At the age of eleven Alan was befriended by an older man "who became a father figure, taking me to ball games, fishing, and other activities. He also introduced me to alcohol, pornography, and he enjoyed performing oral sex on little boys. I didn't like that part, but I figured it was a small price to pay to have a surrogate dad."

Molly: Were you raised with a church background?

Alan: We were active in a large church in Orlando, Florida, that talked about service to God, yet I was not introduced to Jesus Christ. To me, it was more like a social club.

Molly: What happened to your association with the older man?

Alan: It lasted for about six months and then abruptly ended; he disappeared. This relationship left me hurt and vulnerable. Over the next couple of years I experimented with "adult" activities as much as I could. Pornography, tobacco and alcohol always found their way to me, and I was eager to accept them. They made me feel important and wanted.

Molly: Did you continue to associate with homosexuals?

Alan: No. At seventeen I dropped out of school and married a girlfriend whom I had made pregnant. We had what is called an "open relationship" – and both committed adultery at will. On my eighteenth birthday my wife announced she was bisexual and gave me her girlfriend for my birthday present. I thought, "This is great. Now I can live out what I have seen in magazines and fantasized about for years."

We began attending orgies and other illicit parties. After three years of marriage, she walked out one night and never returned.

My life became a whirl of vices including sexual affairs. A woman I met at a bar ended up pregnant and I married once more – another disastrous relationship. We were both heavy drinkers and fought constantly. The day I left was when I was awakened by the sound of a loud click. I looked up to see the barrel of a shotgun poised six inches from my face. My wife had tried to kill me, but had put the wrong shell in the gun!

Molly: Did that experience bring you to your senses?

Alan: It should have, but things became worse. The next woman in my life introduced me to cocaine. It was love at first snort! The drug helped me escape from the disaster my life had become. Soon I was heavily addicted and had to *stay* high. I was snorting so much I was getting massive nosebleeds. Next, I began "booting" – injecting the drug into my veins. For about one minute I became Superman; then I needed another hit, and another, and another.

With my $500-a-day habit, it didn't take long to run out of money. Cocaine had become my god and I would do *anything* to get more. I begged, borrowed, stole, sold everything I possessed and wrote bad checks all over town.

Molly: Did you try to break the drug habit?

Alan: Here's what happened. One fateful day, in October 1990, everything came to a head. I had exhausted my resources of money and no one would accept my checks. Yet, my addiction was so powerful I had to do something.

In desperation, I thought of my childhood and drove to the church where I had grown up. After hearing my story, the pastor said, "I'm sorry I can't help you. Here is the phone number for Narcotics Anonymous. Call us after you get straightened out."

I walked out of the minister's office convinced my fears were confirmed: No one – not even God – loved me. I was totally worthless!

There was only one things to do.
I had to get high! That morning,
I robbed a bank.

Over the next three months I held up a total of four

banks to pay for my drugs. Nothing else mattered to me anymore.

Molly: Didn't you realize that you could have been killed?

Alan: I hated myself and constantly thought about suicide. The gun I carried in the robberies had no bullets, yet I wanted to die. I thought, "When I finally get caught, I will make the cops kill me."

I finally decided to do the job myself. Arranging a place where I would be alone for several hours, I shot the last of my cocaine and swallowed about 50 high blood pressure pills I had stolen from my mother. Then I laid down to die.

Evidently, God had other plans. A woman I was seeing had car trouble and came over to borrow mine. She found me and rushed me to the hospital where they started an IV and hooked me up to an EKG machine.

The last thing I remember was watching the EKG go flat. I thought, "This is it!"

I woke up three days later, miserable. "What a loser! I can't even kill myself!" I thought about jumping from the hospital window, but didn't have the strength to get up.

Molly: Did anyone try to reach you spiritually?

Alan: That same day in the hospital my sister came to see me. She was a Christian, always trying to share Jesus, yet I wouldn't listen. She began telling me again about His peace, joy and love, and I thought, "That's for the *good* people. Not me!"

On my release I was arrested by a detective from the County Sheriff's office on four counts of bank robbery. I soon learned that I was on the Ten Most Wanted list and was in serious trouble.

While the detective was filling out the arrest paperwork at the county jail, something happened that would drastically change the course of my life. Suddenly, he pushed the papers aside, looked me in the eyes and said, "You are going to do some time, but you don't have to do it alone. Jesus loves you and He wants to help you."

Molly: *How did you respond to his statement?*

Alan: Later that night, January 13, 1991, in my jail cell, my mind was reeling. I was thinking about what a mess my life had become and what the officer had said about Jesus. I fell to my knees and cried to the Lord, "If You want my life, You can have it. I'm giving myself to You."

Instantly, the warm peace of God's love washed over me. It was something I had never felt before – and the weight of the world seemed to lift from my shoulders.

God gave me a hunger and love for His Word that rivaled the craving I previously had for drugs.

He set me free from alcohol, cigarettes, hatred, pornography and foul language. I was facing eighty years in prison, yet I was experiencing joy unspeakable.

My lawyer sent me for psychological testing because he thought I was too happy. He called me "The Smiling Bandit."

I was eventually sentenced to 121 months in federal prison – a time that transformed me because of the daily study of God's Word. I became a new man in Christ's image.

In January, 1997, I received a letter from someone I did

not know. After reading it, I handed the letter to my roommate. He looked at it and exclaimed, "Bro, you have just met your wife!"

"I know that, too," I replied. We began to correspond and I asked her to marry me before I even saw her picture. I knew she was the woman God had set aside for me – even though I still faced five more years in prison.

Shortly after we met, a federal sentencing law changed, which reduced my prison time by twenty-one months. That meant I would be free in less than one year.

In the pre-release class, I was told, "Don't expect much of a job when you are first back in society." But I knew the Lord had other plans. He led me to Proverbs 22:1: "A good name is rather to be chosen than great riches."

Molly: How has your life changed?

Alan: The Lord gave me favor with employment and I was married on the day I received my first paycheck. We gave our tithes to God and I was promoted to a supervisory position.

Today my wife and I are involved in ministry as a team. When I think where I was, and where Christ has brought me, I still can't stop smiling!

If we say that we have no sin, we deceive ourselves, and the truth is not in us. If we confess our sins, he is faithful and just to forgive us our sins, and to cleanse us from all unrighteousness.
– 1 John 1:8-9

11

THE CRY OF
AN INNOCENT

*R*hoda clearly remembers the first time her innocence was stripped away. She was only five years old.

"I was awakened in the night, and my clothes were being removed," recalls Rhoda. "I had no idea what my father was doing, yet instinctively I knew I hated the experience."

Her father was also the minister of a local church.

Molly: What did your dad say to you?

Rhoda: The first money I ever received as a child was twenty-five cents. He placed it in my hand and said, "Don't you ever tell anybody about this!"

Of course, I would never tell. He would have killed me!

Molly: What were your feelings at that young age?

Rhoda: I felt confused because my father, the person a child is supposed to love and trust, had deeply wounded me. The abuse continued and I hated him for it.

> *I was extremely fearful and so ashamed I could never put it into words. Every time he approached me, I wanted to run and hide, but it was impossible.*

Molly: Did his advances continue?

Rhoda: As I became older, dad always arranged it so that I would be the one to ride with him to and from church. On those trips he would run his hand up my leg – even offering to give me money if I would fully submit to him.

No one will ever know how difficult it was to sit in the pew and listen to him tell the congregation about living for Christ. He was an excellent preacher and people responded to the message. I now know it was God's Word that touched their hearts, not my father. He disguised his sickness well.

Molly: What else do you recall about your childhood?

Rhoda: In addition to the sexual abuse there were beatings to the point of torture.

I remember the day my sister and I were in trouble for simply going to a neighbor's house without permission and playing with their children. Dad flew into a rage and, as punishment, stuck needles under our fingernails. Then he placed vice grips on our fingers until they turned blue.

Other times we were locked in a dark room and I could

feel the world closing in on us. It was claustrophobia at its worst.

It is a miracle I survived. Once I was beaten with a board that had large nails sticking out of it. The flesh on my hip was ripped open and there were deep holes. I still shudder at the memory.

Several days later my hip became infected and I began running a fever. My dad would hold me down while my mom cleaned out the infection – with alcohol and raw salt.

Molly: *How did you feel about yourself?*

Rhoda: As I entered my teen years I loathed myself even more – believing I was worthless.

> *To the outside world we were the picture of a happy family, yet behind closed doors ours was a house of horrors. I lived in constant fear.*

My father proclaimed to be a Christian, but had some weird beliefs. For example, he once told me, "My spirit can leave my body, and even when I am not near you I can see you at all times." Now I know it was just another ploy to control me.

The abuse increased, and by the time I was fifteen I felt I was losing my mind. His touch made me cringe. Just the sight of him made me physically ill.

Molly: *When did the molestation end?*

Rhoda: One afternoon, still at the age of fifteen, my dad drove me to a graveyard and began to talk about what would happen to me if I were to die. "This is where I would bury your body."

Something inside told me he was serious.

That's when I decided to run away. I shared my plans with some friends at school and they helped me. Unfortunately, they stole the getaway car and we were arrested by the highway patrol. We were sent to a reform school pending a court hearing in my hometown.

One week later a counselor came in and said, "We are taking you home."

That is the last place I wanted to go – imagining the retribution awaiting me.

> *The moment we arrived in our city, I opened up to the police and told them the whole story. They found a family I could live with until the car theft case was settled.*

I was then placed in a foster home.

Molly: *What was ahead on your journey?*

Rhoda: I met my husband when I was fourteen and married him two years later.

In an old country church, at the age of eighteen, I gave my heart to Christ. I realized that even though we are disappointed by those around us, Jesus gave His life to totally redeem us.

Five years later my husband came to the Lord.

Molly: *Tell me about your life today.*

Rhoda: I have been totally delivered and set free of all the pain of my past. If Christ can heal my broken heart, He can heal *anyone.*

Amazing as it may seem, we have been happily married more than thirty years.

> *The Lord has given us a marvelous ministry and we have seen hundreds of lives changed by the power of the Holy Spirit. We want to spend the rest of our lives helping mend broken lives.*

Molly: *Any final words of hope?*

Rhoda: I am only one of thousands of children who are molested and battered every day. Many of these young lives may be in your own neighborhood – even in your church. They are alone, hiding their fear and shame – waiting for someone they can trust to share their agonizing story. Perhaps you may be that person.

God hears the cry of the innocent and He can turn their heartaches into happiness.

~

But as many as received him, to them
gave he power to become the sons of God,
even to them that believe on his name.
— John 1:12

12

Betrayed by Man, Restored by God

*L*uis was only thirteen when he entered a Roman Catholic seminary to become a Franciscan priest. "It was there I began having serious battles with fantasizing and masturbation, says Luis.

When I shared this with my confessor priest, he said, "This is a lonely life, and you need to relax. He began giving me back rubs which led to hugging, kissing, fondling and more."

Molly: Tell me about your early years.

Luis: I was raised in Puerto Rico by my mother. My dad had been absent from my life due to his battles with alcohol. Then he left for the Vietnam conflict.

Starting at the age of ten I developed a fantasy life that focused on the dream of being held securely by strong, masculine men who would show me their affection. That is what I yearned for, yet did not have. When I reached adolescence, the satisfaction I sought in my make-believe

83

world would be accompanied by masturbation.

Molly: Exactly what happened at the seminary?

Luis: I experienced a real sense of loneliness and became attracted to some of my fellow seminarians, and vice-versa, although it was never acted upon.

My confessor priest told me the reason I was having such trouble with masturbation and loneliness. "Luis," he said, "you have been gifted by God with a sense of love that most people do not have."

He explained that he also had a great need for affection, and as a priest he always had to give and give, without ever being on the receiving end." He added, "God wants you to relax and let the tension out of your life."

That is when the back rubs began. Eventually he started to hug and kiss me, and took me to bed where I experienced sex for the first time.

He was a large man, masculine, strong, intelligent and able to protect me – just like my childhood fantasy.

At thirteen I felt I was giving this man of God the love he needed as a servant of the Lord. I enjoyed our intimacy, yet felt what I was doing was wrong. He silenced my fears and I totally submitted to him. Our secret relationship continued several years.

Molly: Did you complete your preparation for ministry?

Luis: No. At the age of twenty-one, after eight years in preparation for the priesthood, I became tired of the hypocrisy and left the seminary.

Now as a university student I no longer had sustained sex with one person. Soon I had multiple partners – even having anonymous sex in bathroom stalls on campus. I started using drugs and began frequenting gay bars, bathhouses and homosexual porno movie houses.

Still, I attempted to lead people into thinking that I was heterosexual, dating girls and even having sex with them. However, men – and drugs – were my main attraction.

Molly: *What about the Lord? Where was He in your life?*

Luis: During this time I met a young man who told me about the saving power of Jesus Christ. Of course, I felt I had already failed the Lord, so why try again?

This born-again believer was persistent and I finally decided to go with him to a church meeting. It was there I committed my life to Christ and immediately returned to my family in Puerto Rico. There I became involved in the church, enrolled in an evangelical Bible institute and began ministering.

Within a few years God blessed me with a wonderful Christian wife and two beautiful daughters. As pastor of a thriving church I was asked to give my testimony at an annual convention of our fellowship, where 3,000 attended.

My pastor friends knew about my Catholic background, the drugs and alcohol, but not about my ex-gay life. For the first time, I shared my complete story and it touched many hearts.

Molly: Were you relieved to finally have your story out in the open?

Luis: I was pleased, yet I was not prepared for the aftermath of my testimony. Almost immediately, pastors who had been so close to me began to shy away. No longer was I receiving calls to participate in the activities of other churches. Even worse, people in my own congregation accused me of preaching false doctrine – yet they had no examples or specifics.

It was becoming obvious to me that the word "gay" drove a bitter wedge – even though it was long ago in my past. There were anonymous insulting phone calls to me and my wife.

I was told by the denomination that I should leave the pastorate, and they sent someone to help me through this supposed "transitional" period in my life. It was useless. My friends in the ministry would not communicate with me.

I found myself becoming angry with everyone – including God.

Molly: What was your next step?

Luis: The situation seemed hopeless and I made the biggest mistake of my life. I reverted to my past. I began drinking again, hanging out in gay baths and acting out homosexual activities. To spare my wife and daughters I thought divorce would be the best solution. I even introduced my wife to my new lover to prove to her it was final.

She was deeply hurt, yet stood firmly on God's Word. She began to earnestly pray for me. "This is a test," she said, "and we will overcome it because God wants our lives to be served for Him."

With Christian compassion she told my lover, "God is not finished with my husband yet."

Molly: Did you listen to your wife?

Luis: Every time I was alone I found myself thinking about passages in the Bible – after all, I knew them by heart. Deep inside I longed to walk with God but felt I had strayed too far.

One afternoon, while visiting our daughters, my wife challenged me. She exclaimed, "Enough is enough! Satan wants to destroy our family and I am not going to let him do it!" She told me, "You are my husband until death. And that's final!"

Then she confirmed her love for me, regardless of the past.

At that moment we both began to pray and cry out to the Lord. I confessed my sin before God and to my wife. I apologized for hurting her so severely and begged her forgiveness.

Molly: What has God taught you from these events?

Luis: Through this experience the secrets of my life finally lost their hold on me. The relationship with my wife grew as never before.

Relocating to Miami, we became involved in a great church, and had counseling that completed a full restoration. Praise God, He has given me a second chance to serve Him! My wife and I are now pastoring a growing congregation.

We may suffer at the hands of men, even within the church. But know this, God has not rejected us. He waits for our repentance and loves us through His son Jesus Christ.

~

Behold, the Lord's hand is not shortened, that it cannot save; neither his ear heavy, that it cannot hear.
– Isaiah 59:1

13

A Purpose for Life

*H*ow does a mother cope when her homosexual son is diagnosed with full blown AIDS? What does she tell him when he has only days to live?

This is the story of Mary, who was forced to face the tragedy millions have encountered – the reality of a child's death.

Molly: Tell me about your son.

Mary: Michael was one of three children, and we raised him in the love of the Lord. As a young boy he was such a delight.

My husband and I have been pastors and evangelists, since we were married, always involved in ministry. My father and grandfather were also preachers.

There was one Scripture I always claimed: "I have no greater joy than to hear that my children walk in truth" (3 John 1:4). You can imagine my dismay when Michael began traveling down a different path.

Molly: When did you first notice that your son was unlike other boys?

Mary: Mothers know their children, and unless they are in total denial, they see the direction their lives are taking. In his pre-teen years my husband and I became concerned about our son's mannerisms, his interests and his friends.

Unbeknown to us, there was a struggle going on inside him that was beyond anything we could comprehend.

When Michael was twelve years old the Lord woke me up one morning and I immediately began to pray for our children, especially him. God spoke to my heart and said, "He is crying out for love, and if he does not find it in the church he is going to go out into the world where he will find love, but it will be counterfeit."

Later, as the years progressed, it became obvious to us that the friends he chose had homosexual tendencies.

Molly: Did you confront him?

Mary: Yes. Our family always had an open relationship and felt we could talk about anything. In 1988, when he was twenty-two, I asked him about the orientation of a particular young man he was spending time with. "Oh, mother," he responded, "he is just a friend. I can't believe you are saying this."

"Michael," I insisted, "you are talking with your mom!" But he was frightened of the truth, afraid we would reject him.

Molly: When did he finally admit his behavior?

Mary: About one year later, when he was diagnosed HIV-positive, he tearfully told us that he was a homosexual.

Molly: *As a mother, how did you deal with that?*

Mary: It was devastating. My whole world just fell apart. "This can't be happening," I cried.

> ## "Michael, where have I failed you?" I asked my son. "What have I done wrong?"

He tried to cushion my grief. "Mother, it's not you. This is just part of *my* life."

At this time he was employed as a flight attendant with a major airline and was afraid of anybody knowing his condition.

I tried to be optimistic, thinking, "This is not the end; we will find a cure. God will take care of him. We are going to make it."

Molly: *How did your husband handle the news?*

Mary: He was humiliated – worried what people would think about a pastor having a child in this lifestyle. Yet he prayed earnestly for his son.

Molly: *What happened next?*

Mary: In 1993 Michael was diagnosed with full blown AIDS. He was horrified and frighted, knowing exactly what he faced. He told me "I am not going to go through the stages of death. I will commit suicide before that."

I responded, "Son, you will go through whatever is necessary because God's grace is sufficient."

"But you don't understand what an AIDS death is like," he said.

I replied, "Maybe I don't have a full understanding, but God said He will be with us until the end."

The Lord was preparing me, giving me strength for the days ahead. It was not long until his condition rapidly declined and he had to leave his work.

Molly: *Did the diagnosis change his spiritual outlook?*

Mary: Absolutely. In 1994, Michael completely surrendered his life back to Christ, began to read his Bible daily and renewed a wonderful relationship with the Lord.

He started watching your "Set Free If You Want to Be" programs on television and said, "Oh, how I would love to attend one of those crusades."

My husband took him and it was a marvelous experience. After the service, one of your assistants walked with him to the front and you ministered to him. He came home and couldn't stop talking about it. "She hugged me and wouldn't let go!" he exclaimed, crying. "I wanted to pull back, but she wouldn't let me. For the first time I felt the love of God go completely through me."

Molly: *What was it like to see him fail physically?*

Mary: In 1995, we were by Michael's side in the hospital night and day as he battled various infections. Over his bed we hung a banner, "God is in control."

One day, my sister and her two daughters arrived. For twelve years our relationship had been broken and God used this event to mend the shattered areas of our lives. From that moment, they were there for us constantly.

Our older son, who had a total disdain for the lifestyle his brother had chosen, walked into the room and there was a total healing and restoration in our family.

When we were alone, I said:

> *"Michael, do you realize what purpose you are fulfilling in this family? He nodded his head and said, "Yes, mother. I see."*

Molly: *What was your prayer for him?*

Mary: When Michael had practically no strength left in his body, I began to ask him to repeat a ten-finger prayer with me every day. It was the ten words of Philippians 4:13: "I can do all things through Christ which strengtheneth me."

Each day, he would hold up one finger at a time and utter that prayer. Even when his condition had weakened to the point where he could only speak in a whisper, he would say those words to the Lord.

Molly: *What have you learned from this experience?*

Mary: On April 19, 1995, I watched Michael leave this earth, and that same verse from Philippians came alive in my own spirit. It is only the Lord who gives me the courage and strength to continue.

There have been days of emotional grief and pain, yet we rejoice in knowing that Michael is with the Lord.

Now I can speak for someone whose voice has been silenced. Regardless of what you face, there is a purpose for your life.

~

Lo, children are an heritage of the
Lord: and the fruit of the womb is his reward.
– Psalms 127:3

14

RELEASED FROM REBELLION

*M*ike was raised in a Godly home in Indonesia, the son of missionaries. "I was only five years old when I was first molested by a trusted member of the staff at the school where my parents were dorm supervisors," recalls Mike. "It was the beginning of a long downward spiral."

Molly: What was your reaction when the molestation began?

Mike: At first I resisted, hardly knowing what was happening. But as the sexual acts continued I became willingly involved. It went on for several years, and my parents had no idea what was taking place.

When I was ten years old, our family left Indonesia after seventeen years of ministry and permanently returned to the United States, living in Florida.

Molly: Since you were still young, were you able to block out what happened and move on with your life?

Mike: I wish that were true, but even at the age of ten the seeds of rebellion were already sown. I was upset about everything – including the fact that I had been uprooted from my childhood home. My anger was directed at my parents, and at God.

Molly: How did this resentment begin to show itself?

Mike: At first, my rebellion surfaced by disobeying my parents at every opportunity. Then, as I reached my teen years, I began smoking and experimenting with anything my mom and dad considered "wrong." Because of what occurred in Indonesia, I had a sexual curiosity beyond my years, and became obsessed with pornography. I was constantly stealing porn magazines from neighborhood stores.

Molly: Did you tell anyone about the molestation that had taken place?

Mike: No. I was too ashamed to reveal what happened. Looking back, I should have brought it to light, because it affected me so deeply. As a result of my silence, it festered and erupted into many negative activities. By the time my parents noticed the change in me, I was engulfed in so much anger that I didn't want their help. I rejected their love and was determined to do it my way?

Molly: Where did the rebellion lead?

Mike: By the time I was eighteen my life was a constant cycle of pot, parties, drinking and sex. Anyway I could hurt my parents, that's what I did.

> *After I had been arrested four times*
> *for various thefts, my parents made a*
> *decision I am sure was difficult for them*
> *– they kicked me out of the house.*

Molly: *Where did you go? How did you live?*

Mike: I started aimlessly roaming from town to town, state to state, obviously trying to escape the pain I felt inside. I worked at odd jobs and spent the money on drugs.

At every turn I would get into more trouble and quickly move on. During this time I lived in constant rebellion and didn't see my parents for one year.

In Houston, I stole the car of a guy I was living with and took off for Wisconsin. I was arrested and placed in jail for eight months.

Molly: *Did being in prison bring you to your senses?*

Mike: Only partially. My parents made contact with me while I was incarcerated and, after my release, I went to live with them in Florida – pretending I had changed my ways.

Severely addicted to alcohol and pornography, I soon found myself slipping back into a cycle of sin. My concerned parents confronted me and I was asked to leave home once more.

Immediately, I headed for a bar where I met a man I had previously known. "Why don't you come and live with me?" he asked.

Since I could not keep a job, this seemed like a good alternative. The man was gay and let me know that if I wanted to stay around – and have the drugs and alcohol he provided – I would need to be part of his life, sexually. At twenty-one years old, hanging out in gay bars became the norm. I was out of control.

Molly: Could you see where this was taking you? Did you think about turning your life around?

Mike: There were times I desperately wanted to change, but knew my shortcomings. I was weak, and too stubborn to ask God to transform me. I would think about the religious training I had as a child, and quickly dismiss it from my mind.

At one time I looked up to God, clenched my fist and said, "I hate You! I told Him, "I am giving my life to Satan." When that happened, it seemed I no longer had the slightest control over my actions, and I fell deeper into the pit of perversion.

I didn't know it at the time, but my mother was on her knees every night, praying that God would bring me back. She also formed prayer teams, each praying for me on specific days of the week.

Molly: What was the result of those prayers?

Mike: At the lowest point on my journey, when I was thinking about ending my life, God clearly spoke to me. He said, "You can either die in what you are doing, or you can choose life."

It was as if a lightbulb clicked on inside me. For the first time I felt a glimmer of hope. Immediately I found a pastor and told him everything about my past – everything, including my molestation as a child. At that point it didn't matter who knew, I had abused my life so much, something had to change.

The minister told me about a residency program I should consider and I made the phone call. They said, "We would love to have you, but you must *want* to change. It has to be your decision."

"I am ready," I told them.

Molly: How did the program affect you?

Mike: Two weeks after moving to the facility, my parents came for a visit. It was difficult for me to face them, knowing how much hurt and shame I had brought into their lives. We cried and prayed together and God began a great work of healing.

The ten-month program was amazing. I totally re-dedicated my life to the Lord and experienced His regeneration process.

> *God took the strongholds of anger and fear and replaced them with His love.*

Eventually, I wrote letters of forgiveness to every person I had harmed along the way.

Molly: *What do you see for your future?*

Mike: The Lord delivered me from my past for a purpose. I plan to spend the rest of my life helping others. If God opens the doors, I would love to return to Indonesia as a missionary.

~

*Then will I sprinkle clean water upon you,
and ye shall be clean: from all your filthiness,
and from all your idols, will I cleanse you. A new
heart also will I give you, and a new spirit will I put
within you: and I will take away the stony heart
out of your flesh, and I will give you an heart of
flesh. And I will put my spirit within you, and
cause you to walk in my statutes, and ye shall
keep my judgments, and do them.*
– Ezekiel 36:25-27

15

THE DRUG STORE

*J*anet was an innocent thirteen-year-old in Michigan when she began her first job – running the soda fountain, selling cards and candy, and stocking the shelves in the small town's drug store.

As Janet recalls it, "When the soda containers became low or empty I had to go to the basement to get more stock. And soon after I started my job the store owner followed me down the stairs and began to sexually molest me."

It was an activity that didn't stop for nearly five years!

Molly: What was your response to his first advances? Did you protest? Did you tell your parents?

Janet: It was my mother's idea that I take the job. You see, I was rather shy and she thought it would be great if I got out and met people in a work situation.

When the sexual advances began, I was frightened, confused, and ashamed to tell *anyone* what was happening.

Knowing my mother didn't handle things well, I thought, "She will just go to pieces." So I didn't tell her for more than a year.

Molly: *What did she say when you finally broke the news?*

Janet: The store owner was not only a respected man in the community, he was also a friend of our family. When I finally gathered the strength to tell her what was happening, I wasn't prepared for her response. "You're lying," she protested. "I don't believe a word of it!"

Even more, she said, "I don't want you to ever say a thing like that again." Mom wouldn't even consider the idea that I stop working for the man.

Molly: *You said you were rather shy as a girl. Tell me about your childhood.*

Janet: When I was very young I was adopted into a family who had a child of their own – two years older than me. My sister constantly told me, "You don't belong in this family," and made my life miserable. She would tease me and it made me feel I was not really loved.

My mother would care for me, but I did not feel a close bond of love.

Feelings of rejection led to my continual desire to run and hide. The closest relationship was with my father, but when he worked nights or was out of the house I would head for the basement or close myself in my room.

Molly: *How long did you stay at the job in the drug store?*

Janet: Every time I went to work I felt sick and fearful, yet I saw no way out. I just closed my mind to what was taking place – and the molestation continued.

I kept working for the man until the day I finished high school. I also remember the gift he gave me at graduation – a white Bible. What nerve!

Molly: What affect did these years have on you?

Janet: Since the drug store owner was an older man and I was so young, he made it feel it was *my* fault this was happening. He boosted my ego, telling me how beautiful I was, and that it was what I wanted.

Looking back, I see how it broke my spirit and caused me to do things I should not have done.

In high school I became promiscuous, and at the age of seventeen gave birth to a child. I gave her up for adoption, feeling even more unworthy.

Molly: What about marriage?

Janet: While still in my teens I married a man who joined the military and eventually became a police officer. He was extremely controlling and wouldn't allow me to make friends with anyone. Part of it was my fault. I thought, "If they knew about my past they would turn their backs on me."

When people reached out to me, I would create a barrier and push them away.

Eventually he left me for another woman. Again, I was rejected.

Molly: What was it like to be deserted?

Janet: For an entire year after he left, I spent most of my time in bed, crying. I thought, "Surely, he will come back."

I lost considerable weight and couldn't cope with life. I learned later the man became an alcoholic and lost his job.

One day I received a phone call that he had taken his life. It seemed that pain followed me wherever I traveled.

Molly: Was there any hope on your horizon?

Janet: My life was dominated by rage and resentment. Then one day, after moving to a new apartment, I was unpacking a box and picked up the white Bible I had been given by the man who molested me. Slowly, I opened the pages.

> *Instantly, I was overcome with emotion. My hands started to shake and I began to sob, uncontrollably.*

I found a chair and cried out to the Lord, "I cannot live with this anger anymore. God, You've got to do something. Please, Lord!"

Suddenly, I felt something heavy in the pit of my stomach. It was like a brick that was stirring around. Then, in a moment, I felt it leaving me – like someone had taken it and thrown it out of my body!

Even though I had not been a church-going person, I knew without a doubt that God was doing a healing work. As I began to read that Bible, all the bitterness and hurt I had carried for so many years began to vanish. The Lord set me free!

Molly: Did spiritual matters become a major force in your life from that moment on?

Janet: It didn't happen instantly since church was not part of my culture. However, God was at work. He sent another man into my life who had a wonderful relationship with the Lord – far deeper than my own. We had a daughter together.

One Saturday night he asked, "Will you go to church with me tomorrow morning?"

Being a good wife, I responded, "Of course!"

We attended on Sunday Morning and he was anxious to go back that same night. Then he was ready to attend Wednesday night Bible study. "Isn't this a little too much?" I said.

A few days later, he called me from work and said, "I want you to be dressed to go to church tonight."

I responded, "On Friday?" I thought that was supposed to be "date" night – dinner and dancing.

"They are having a revival at the church and I told the pastor we would be there," said my husband.

Since I didn't want to stay home alone, I went to the service.

What a night it was! For the first time I felt the anointing of God's Holy Spirit come over me and I totally rededicated my life to Christ.

Molly: How did God help you bury the pieces of your past?

Janet: The relationship with my mother was totally restored. She had been in denial about the man who owned the drug store, but later learned he had preyed on another girl when he owned a store in a neighboring town.

My second daughter searched for the girl I had given up for adoption – and found her. We had a wonderful reunion that has resulted in an ongoing relationship.

The unpleasant parts of my past are buried and only the good remains. The Lord has given my husband and I a ministry together and we will spend the rest of our lives reaching out to those who are hurting. It's amazing!

~

Heal me, O Lord, and I shall be healed; save
me, and I shall be saved: for thou art my praise.
– Jeremiah 17:14

16

"How Can it be Wrong?"

*D*an was about fourteen years old when it hit him that he was different from other boys. He said to himself, "You are gay! You are homosexual!" – and he hated himself for it, not wanting to be that way.

As strange as it may seem, Dan never met anyone else in the lifestyle until he was twenty years old. He lived in a small farming community where, "there was no one around who was like me."

Molly: What was it like at home?

Dan: My dad, the son of an alcoholic, worked two jobs to support the family and I seldom saw him. At home he was usually too tired to spend time with me so we really never had much of a relationship.

Mother was the head of the household. She was domineering, and drunk most of the time.

I was the youngest of four children and we didn't have

107

the basic training we needed. What we learned was on our own or from other kids at school.

Both of my parents were very heavy into alcohol and I suffered physical abuse from my mother and emotional neglect from my dad. They divorced when I was sixteen.

Molly: Did your family attend church?

Dan: No. I don't ever remember them talking to me about God. And there was no Bible in our home.

My only spiritual training was what I received from the Catholic school I attended. I developed a desire to know God and went to Mass on weekends – by myself.

However, I didn't really understand what the priests were saying, and never had a personal relationship with the Lord. I just went through the ritual.

Molly: Did you like girls when you were growing up?

Dan: Sometimes yes, and sometimes no. It was around the third or fourth grade when I began being attracted to boys.

About the same time I heard about homosexuality – that it was wrong, a perversion, sick, and that you would burn in Hell if you behaved that way!"

It seemed that every time I turned around a lustful thought would enter my mind or there was an action I didn't know how to control. I tried to stop it, but couldn't. It led to a drug and alcohol addiction by the age of sixteen.

Most of the teens I hung around with were female – I felt more comfortable with them. The young men were into sports and cars, and that wasn't me.

Molly: Where did you turn for answers?

Dan: Because of my curiosity, I found a Bible and learned what it said about homosexuality – that God was totally against it. Then I visited several denominational churches and their interpretation was different; very tolerant on the topic.

Here was my own analysis:

> *"If this is the way I am, how can it be wrong? I've done everything I can do to change and I am still the same. Why would God make me this way?"*

Molly: Did you keep your sexual orientation a secret?

Dan: By the time I was twenty-one I was driving to larger cities and meeting other homosexuals. I also decided to "come out" and let people – even in my home town know about my life.

During this time there was a series of men in my circle who would stay for two weeks or two months, seldom longer. I had companionship, yet was always lonely and never satisfied. There was always a void, an empty space inside.

It led to substance abuse, eating disorders and new-age religious practices.

Before long I felt myself slipping into a state of depression and checked myself into a psychiatric hospital.

Molly: What did you learn at the hospital?

Dan: They taught the basics of self-esteem; how to make yourself number one in your life. They told me, "Take control and become your own god. Make personal choices and don't let people tell you what to do."

Later, I found a therapist who helped me understand what happened to me in my childhood. It confirmed what I already knew – that the love and security I lacked from my father I was seeking from other men. Still, I could not find it.

Molly: *What was your next step?*

Dan: I became an activist. I thought that if I were the only gay person in my community, there must be other lonely gay individuals in the surrounding towns. I spread the word and started a support group with weekly meetings and monthly activities. I also became the spokesperson for a gay and lesbian crisis line, speaking on behalf of homosexual rights.

However, even that activity didn't give me satisfaction. After the program had been in operation for about a year I handed the keys to an associate.

Molly: *Did that mean your giving up your gay life?*

Dan: No. I was confused and traveled to Florida for a two week vacation, to do some thinking. While I was there, the night before I was to return home, on the beach I heard what I felt was God speaking to me – something extremely unusual in my experience.

He seemed to be telling me to move to Florida, and that "I have a plan for your life."

At the time I was struggling to exit the lifestyle, but didn't know how.

Molly: *Did you obey what God said?*

Dan: I made the move to Florida but, like a magnet, the homosexual bars drew me in. Within a short time the feelings of anxiety and depression began to resurface and I said to myself, "This is it! I've got to get out of this life once and for all!"

There was no one I really cared for and I decided to return to my hometown. At that same time, God placed someone in my path who began talking to me about Jesus."

At first I thought, "Not another religious kook!" but there was something diffcrent about this person. In my heart I knew it was the answer I had always needed – I longed to know the truth.

Two days later I went to church with the individual and dedicated my life to Christ.

Molly: *Tell me about the change that took place.*

Dan: It wasn't like an instant bolt of lightning. I struggled for another six months with my inner feelings, avoiding the bars, reading my Bible and going to church.

In my limited understanding, I thought the things I had done were too shameful for the Lord to really love and forgive me. It reached the point where I said, "God, either totally deliver me or take me now!"

At that moment I clearly heard a voice telling me, "Turn on the television."

When I clicked the button there was the theme song to your program, "Set Free!" I can't even remember who you interviewed, but as I watched, I knew the great void in my life was starting to be filled.

I phoned your ministry and we prayed together.

Since that time God has given me a vision for my future and has blessed me beyond measure. Not only has He totally taken my homosexual desires away, he brought a beautiful woman in my life and we plan to spend our lives together.

~

Because he hath set his love upon me, therefore
will I deliver him: I will set him on high, because
he hath known my name. He shall call upon me, and
I will answer him: I will be with him in trouble; I
will deliver him, and honor him. With long life
will I satisfy him, and show him my salvation.
– Psalms 91:14-16

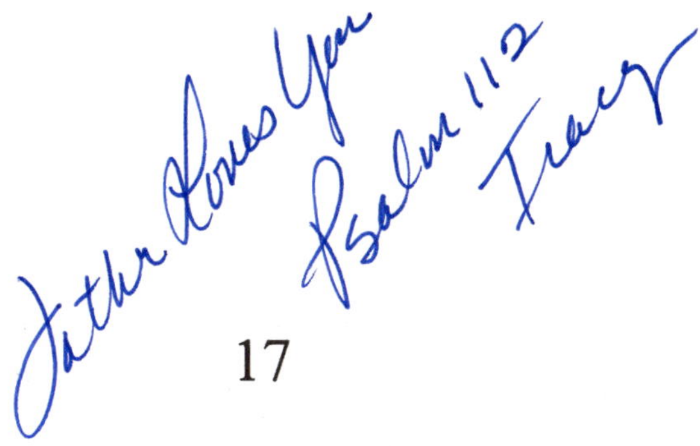

17

DEMONS, DRUGS AND DELIVERANCE

*I*n Key West, Florida, Tracy hit rock bottom. "Every day I was freebasing and shooting cocaine," she says. "After a sordid life, I hated myself and was ready to end it all. No one really cared about me."

At that moment, someone knocked on the door of her small house trailer with an invitation that would dramatically change her future.

Molly: Let's start at the beginning. What happened during your childhood?

Tracy: I was only five years old when my dad left my mom in Taylor, Michigan, near Detroit. Mom was a wonderful Christian who took me to church and we would pray together.

However, something occurred when I was in the second grade that would drastically change the course of my life. I was at a Brownie meeting and my mother didn't come to

113

pick me up. I called her but the phone went dead. So I reached my grandfather, who arrived to take me home.

As we came close to our neigborhood I could see fire trucks on the street and smoke billowing to the sky. "That's *our* house," I screamed as we drew near.

My mother burned to death in that fire on January 2, 1971. They found her on the kitchen floor with the phone in her hand – I was sure she had answered the phone just as I hung up.

Even worse, I remembered the last words I spoke to my mother before leaving for school that same morning. We had an argument about some trivial matter and I bellowed, "I hate you. I wish you were dead!"

Those words would haunt me for the next twenty-four years.

Molly: *Where did you go? Who raised you?*

Tracy: I was taken away by my father, who lived in Pittsburgh, Pennsylvania. He was the exact opposite of my mom, and lived far away from God.

Almost immediately, I began to hate my life, thinking I had killed the only person in the whole world who really loved me. I closed my heart to everyone and walked through the motions.

I even hated God for what had happened!

I thought, "Why should I get close to anyone? They will be taken away!"

At the age of ten I began smoking and drinking – especially vodka. I would steal it from my father. The alcohol seemed to take away the hurt.

The same year I was stealing so much that I was ordered to write, "Thou shalt not steal" a thousand times.

My father was into the occult and taught me how to chant and pray to Druid and Greek gods. We played with the pyramid and trusted tarot cards to direct our future. I learned to use the ouija board and began to channel spirit guides. I was fascinated by all of this, yet fearful.

From the age of ten I was having sex with other girls and into really heavy petting with boys.

By the time I was thirteen my father and his new wife would dress me up and take me to the bars. I would drink the night away with them. Drugs were part of the atmosphere and I would bring my dad bags of pot and quaaludes. Even at this young age, I was extremely well developed and fully sexually active.

Molly: *Where did this life lead you?*

Tracy: I ran away from home when I was fourteen – passing for twenty-three. With a fake ID, I began to work as a stripper in Pennsylvania, West Virginia, Ohio and New York. I danced on the circuit for years.

When I was seventeen I went to Myrtle Beach, South Carolina for a vacation. It was there I met my first husband and we were together for ten years.

At twenty-three in the hospital with a threat of cancer, I was given a massive hysterectomy. During my marriage, I was never faithful to my husband – and he knew it. We divorced in 1991.

Molly: *What was the next stop on your journey?*

Tracy: I headed for New Orleans, saying to myself, "I'm going there to die." Over the years I had many dreams of death and knew it was on the horizon.

In this city of sin, I began to learn more about witchcraft. I worked in the bars in the "graveyard shift" – from midnight until four o'clock in the morning. This is when the nastiest people come out to play. My friends were into demons, evil spirits and the occult.

I played with the girls and the boys – and the boys who were girls! It was a blurry time because of the booze, the drugs and witchcraft. I had a hard time keeping a job because the party never stopped.

Molly: How long did you stay in New Orleans?

Tracy: About eight months into my life in the French Quarter, I put my hooks into some sicko from up north and left with him. Of course, that didn't work out. After a month I left and made my way to Jacksonville, Florida. It was there I caught the eye of another fellow and we went to the Florida Keys.

After leaving him I parked my stuff in a little trailer behind a Key West bar and called it home. There were plenty of people to take with a flip of the hair and a wink of the eye. I could tell a good lie and there were guys and gals to be had everywhere.

Still, I had the garbage of my past to deal with.

The next three years were a blur – lost to the drug needle and uncounted gallons of booze. The demons in my life were demanding a commitment and I was tormented night and day. It reached a point where I would try to go and get picked up at a club but men and women wanted nothing to do with me. I was a violent partner.

I moved in with a guy strictly because he had a job and I wanted his money for drugs. I hated his touch, but needed the cocaine to keep the demons quiet.

Molly: What happened that changed your situation?

Tracy: About 11 A.M. on a Friday I sat in my stench on the pull-out sofa in my little house trailer.

I looked in the mirror and hated what I saw.

Yet, I was stuck with nowhere to go and no one to help me. My beauty had faded with the years of abuse and I had no veins left to stick a needle. I was finished.

For the first time in years I began to pray. "God," I cried, "I can't handle this anymore. It's too big for me. Please, if You are still there take this weight from off my shoulders. I need You!"

At that very moment a knock came to my door. It was a minister from a small church in Key West. He and a young boy invited me to a movie they were having and said there would be snacks afterward. It sounded good; I could use some food.

I walked into that little church and saw people who were smiling – they were happy! After the film, "The Sound of Distant Thunder," the pastor gave an invitation. "If you want to have a new life in Jesus, come to the front. We want to pray with you."

That was it! I needed this Jesus. I knew Him as a child and realized I still loved Him.

As I stood to my feet and started down that aisle, I felt I was being attacked by Satan himself. I was gripped with fear and my whole body was shaking. In my head the devil was screaming, "No! I will kill you! I won't let Him take you!"

Molly: Did you listen to Satan?

Tracy: What did I have to lose? When I finally got to the front I was crying uncontrollably and wailing for my sin. I was filthy, and had done things even the most wicked would find horrific. Yet, there I stood before a Holy God.

On that night, October, 19, 1995 at 8:23 P.M., the Lord heard the cry of my heart and forgave me completely!

Much has taken place since that wonderful night. I was delivered of every demon and evil habit. He healed me of hepatitis and liver disease.

Even greater, I am now married to a mighty man of God and we are sharing the Good News of Christ.

Jesus took the chaos of my life and made me a daughter of the most High God. I am free!

~

When my father and my mother forsake me, then the Lord will take me up. . .Hear, O Lord, when I cry with my voice: have mercy also upon me, and answer me.
— Psalms 27:10,7

18

STAYING FREE!

I have spent hours talking with men and women who have come out of the lifestyle, yet sadly returned to their old ways. One man cried, "Molly, when I went back, it was worse than ever before. The craving for sexual desires seemed to intensify!"

Satan loves an empty house. He sends ungodly friends to tempt you back into sin. You'll hear the voices luring, "Oh, it is so good to see you. I've missed you so much!"

Jesus spoke to this situation. He said, "When an evil spirit comes out of a man, it goes through arid places seeking rest and does not find it. Then it says, 'I will return to the house I left.' When it arrives, it finds the house unoccupied, swept clean and put in order. Then it goes and takes with it seven other spirits more wicked than itself, and they go in and live there. And the final condition of that man is worse than the first. That is how it will be with this wicked generation" (Matthew 12:43-45 NIV).

When there is a void, something – or *someone* – will attempt to fill it.

Don't expect Satan to leave you alone. When Jesus went to

the wilderness to fast and pray, Satan was there. The Bible records that "...when the devil had ended all the temptation, he departed from him for a season" (Luke 4:13). It wasn't a permanent departure – only for a period of time.

What should you do when the devil entices you? Follow the example of Jesus. He said, "Get thee behind me, Satan: for it is written, Thou shalt worship the Lord thy God, and him only shalt thou serve" (v.8).

Jesus used the Word of God – "It is written!"

Seven Steps

While reading the stories in this book perhaps you have said to yourself, "I wish that I could be like those people. Oh, how I would love to break free from my past and have a new beginning."

You can!

> *Not only can you become*
> *free – you can stay free!*

After asking Jesus to be your Savior and making a commitment to Him, here are seven steps I would like to share with you. I feel they will help you build a new life.

1. Forgive any person who has harmed you.

It may be someone who molested or raped you, or led you into homosexuality or drugs. Even if the offending person is your father, mother or a family member, you must forgive.

Perhaps you are saying, " Molly, you don't know what I went through? I'm not sure they *deserve* my pardon."

It is time to bury your feelings and follow the command of

Jesus. He said, "For if you forgive men when they sin against you, your heavenly Father will also forgive you. But if you do not forgive men their sins, your Father will not forgive your sins" (Matthew 6:14-15).

Forgiveness is an act of God's grace being poured upon you by His Spirit. It is a vital part of healing and restoration.

2. Eliminate pornography.

If there is any suggestive or graphic reading material in your possession, get ride of it immediately. If you have been addicted to pornography, destroy the videos and magazines.

We are told to "Hate what is evil; cling to what is good" (Romans 12:9). Ask the Lord to cleanse your mind of every evil image and wash away every lustful thought.

Meditate on what Christ did for you on the Cross so that you can be totally liberated!

3. Renounce masturbation.

This behavior can be active in a person's life for many reasons. Ask the Holy Spirit to show you the root causes and the process through which you can expect deliverance and healing.

Paul wrote, "It is God's will that you should be sanctified ...that each of you should learn to control his own body in a way that is holy and honorable" (1 Thessalonians 4:4 NIV).

Masturbation can be a work of the enemy. He would rather have you fulfilled in *yourself* than in marriage. Renounce it. Make a final decision to let the matter be settled with God – that it will no longer be an option in your life.

The Bible says that in the last days, "...men shall be lovers of their own selves...Without natural affection...lovers of pleasures more than lovers of God" (2 Timothy 3:2-4).

4. Separate yourself from your lover.

After many years in ministry I have seen first hand what happens when two lives become entwined. When a person touches your body a web starts to weave – and can lead to the buying of homes, cars and investments together. Then, when one of the partners comes to Christ and tries to escape, they realize they are snared in a web.

A hairdresser in New York City was marvelously converted after being with his lover for eighteen years. The Lord so convicted him of his lifestyle that he walked away from his business with the man – even giving him the car they jointly owned. He told me, "I wouldn't trade my peace with my God for anything."

The Bible says, "Wherefore come out from among them, and be ye separate, saith the Lord, and touch not the unclean thing; and I will receive you" (2 Corinthians 6:17).

5. Reject condemnation.

Attempting to tell a nonbeliver about the transformation in your life can be a challenge.

When people ridicule your decision to live for the Lord and remark, "You'll be back," read the words of Paul: "Therefore, there is now no condemnation for those who are in Christ Jesus, because through Christ Jesus the law of the Spirit of life set me free from the law of sin and death" (Romans 8:1-2).

Why don't your former friends understand what has taken place? It is because "...the natural man receiveth not the things of the Spirit of God: for they are foolishness unto him: neither can he know them, because they are spiritually discerned" (1 Corinthians 2:14).

Your decision to follow the Lord far outweighs any condemnation that may cross your path.

6. Develop a relationship with Christ.

There are two important ways you can have fellowship with the Lord: (1) through prayer, and (2) by reading His Word.

Set a specific time each day to commune with your Heavenly Father. Don't burden Him with requests, rather talk with Him as a personal friend.

Open your Bible and start reading. The book of John in the New Testament is an excellent place to begin. When you find a verse that has special meaning for you, memorize it – then speak it out loud.

Allow the Word to become buried deep inside you and let it penetrate your very soul.

Practice *confessing* God's promises. With His help you will keep your deliverance and become a total, complete person in Christ.

Also develop a relationship with God's people. Find a church home and a pastor to whom you are accountable. The Bible tells us to, "Obey them that have the rule over you, and submit yourselves: for they watch for your souls" (Hebrews 13:17).

7. Praise and worship the Lord.

Finally, spend time praising God – not only in a church, but in your private time. If you desire for the Lord to restore your health and emotions, praise Him for what He is already doing. Say, "Father, I praise you for healing my body, for restoring my mind, for allowing me to forgive others who have hurt me and taken advantage of my life."

You are being renewed and regenerated when you allow God to cleanse you through adoration and worship.

I suggest that you listen to recordings produced by

companies such as Hosanna! Music and Vineyard.

The psalmist wrote, "Let every thing that hath breath praise the Lord. Praise ye the Lord" (Psalms 150:6).

My Prayer for You

I want to express my thanks to you for taking the time to read this book. If it has touched your life in any way, I am asking you to say this prayer with me:

Dear Jesus, I confess with my mouth and believe in my heart that you died on the Cross for my sin. I am asking You to cleanse me with Your precious blood and forgive me of every transgression of my life.

I pray by your Holy Spirit that Your anointing will flow over me and that you will break my stony heart and give me a heart of flesh. Remove every sinful desire from my life.

Lord I am bringing to you every act that has been committed against me and every sin of my life. Bury them in the sea of forgetfulness and give me a brand new start. As I ask you to forgive me, I also forgive every person who has harmed me.

Father, I am making a covenant with You that never again will I return to a life that is displeasing to You. I promise to read Your Word, to pray and to fellowship with believers.

Thank You Lord, for saving me, cleansing me, and setting me free. I pray this in Jesus' name. Amen.

Remember, Jesus loves you, and so do I – You are special. If you have not had a hug today, here is my hug to you. I love you!

If the Son therefore shall make
you free, ye shall be free indeed.
– John 8:36

RECOMMENDED RESOURCES

The Broken Image, Leanne Payne (Grand Rapids, MI: Baker Book House, 1996). Includes case histories of those with sexual identity disorders.

Coming Out of Homosexuality, Bob Davies and Lori Rentzel (Downers Grove, IL: InterVarsity Press, 1993). This book deals with breaking addictive patterns and changing self-identity.

Desires in Conflict, Joe Dallas (Eugene, OR: Harvest House Publishers, 1991). Effective help for restoring sexual wholeness.

The Healing of the Homosexual, Leanne Payne (Grand Rapids, MI: Baker Book House, 1996). The role of prayer in healing broken lives.

Out of Egypt: Leaving Lesbianism Behind, Jeanette Howard (Crowborough, England: Monarch Publications, 1991). Deals specifically with the healing of the lesbian.

Pursuing Sexual Wholeness: How Jesus Heals the Homosexual, Andrew Comiskey (Lake Mary, FL: Creation House, 1989). An outstanding volume we highly recommend.

Sexual Healing: God's Plan for the Sanctification of Broken Lives, David Kyle Foster (Jacksonville, FL: Mastering Life Ministries, 1995). A reference manual for those trapped in sexual sin and brokenness.

Someone I Love is Gay: How Family and Friends Can Respond, Anita Worthen and Bob Davies (Downers Grove, IL: InterVarsity Press, 1996). Excellent resource for parents and friends of a homosexual.

SEXUAL ADDICTION

A Way of Escape, Neil T. Anderson (Eugene, OR: Harvest House Publishers, 1994). An excellent resource for those who are struggling with sexual strongholds in the mind.

An Affair of the Mind, Laurie Hall (Colorado Springs, CO: Focus on the Family Publishers, 1996). Deals with pornography addiction.

Don't Call it Love: Recovery from Sexual Addiction, Patrick Carnes (New York: Bantam Books, 1991). A thorough examination of the topic from a secular point of view.

False Intimacy: Understanding the Struggle of Sexual Addiction, Dr. Harry Schaumburg (Colorado Springs, CO: NavPress, 1992). A highly acclaimed book dealing with the core issues of sexual addiction.

SEXUAL ABUSE OF CHILDREN

Child Sexual Abuse, Maxine Hancock and Karen Mains (Wheaton, IL: Harold Shaw Publishers, 1987). Practical advice on how to work through the steps of recovery and forgiveness.

The Wounded Heart: Hope for Adult Victims of Childhood Sexual Abuse, Dr. Dan B. Allender (Colorado Springs, CO: NavPress, 1990) . God's path to healing for those who have been sexually violated.

What *to Do When You Find Out Your Wife Was Sexually Abused,* John Courtright and Dr. Sid Rogers (Grand Rapids, MI: Zondervan, 1994). An insightful volume directed to husbands who are tying to cope with the confusion, fear and anger that result when their wives first confront and then begin to recover from past abuse.

To Contact
Molly International Ministries
or
Set Free if You Want to Be

Write: Box 2068, Largo, FL 33779-2068
Phone: 727-586-3733
Fax: 737-586-2649
E-mail: setfreeif@ij.net
Internet: www.setfreeif.org